D0216485

Moving and Shaking American Medicine

**Recent Titles in
Contributions in Economics and Economic History**

Moving and Shaking American Medicine

THE STRUCTURE OF A SOCIOECONOMIC TRANSFORMATION

Betty Leyerle

CONTRIBUTIONS IN ECONOMICS AND ECONOMIC
HISTORY, NUMBER 57
GREENWOOD PRESS
WESTPORT, CONNECTICUT · LONDON, ENGLAND

Library of Congress Cataloging in Publication Data

Leyerle, Betty.
  Moving and shaking American medicine.

  (Contributions in economics and economic history,
ISSN 0084-9235 ; no. 57)
  Bibliography: p.
  Includes index.
  1. Medical economics—United States.   2. Social
medicine—United States.   I. Title.   II. Series.
[DNLM: 1. Health policy—United States.   2. Health
services—Trends—United States.   3. Socioeconomic
factors.   W84 AA1 L64m]
RA410.7.L48   1984   362.1′0973   83-22646
ISBN 0-313-24020-5 (lib. bdg.)

Library of Congress Catalog Card Number: 83-22646
ISBN: 0-313-24020-5
ISSN: 0084-9235

First published in 1984

Greenwood Press
A division of Congressional Information Service, Inc.
88 Post Road West, Westport, Connecticut 06881

Printed in the United States of America

10 9 8 7 6 5 4 3 2 1

Contents

Contents   vii

Moving and Shaking American Medicine

1

Introduction

During the mid–1970's, observers representing an astonishing range of political and philosophical colorations came to agree that a crisis existed in the American health care system. Their definitions of major problems were varied. Occupational and environmental health activists thought the emphasis by the medical establishment on curative rather than preventive medicine masked the social causes of disease; they were outraged that the Occupational Safety and Health Administration (OSHA), several years after its creation, was still using standards set by industry and that even those were inadequately enforced. Women's groups had been complaining for a decade that physicians practiced sexist medicine, including overutilization of surgical procedures on women; they advocated and taught various kinds of "self-help." The poor, who had historically been denied access to basic health care services, had finally gained it through passage of Medicare and Medicaid in the mid–1960's, only to see major scandals erupt in the press shortly thereafter. These scandals involved both accusations of fraud and abuse by physicians and suggestions that the human rights of poor patients were violated through punitive sterilizations and improper experimentation in teaching hospitals.

Everybody, especially corporate executives and government officials, was appalled by the degree of inflation in the health care sector, where costs rose from $39 billion to $160 billion between the time Medicare and Medicaid became effective and 1977. A study commissioned by the Department of Health, Education, and Welfare (HEW) predicted that by the year 2000 the direct costs of health care in the United States would be more than $1 trillion annually; the total costs, including loss of earning power, would be more than twice that amount.[1]

To complicate matters further, there was no agreement about whether or not these astronomical costs were excessive. Access to health care had so recently been extended to the elderly and poor that no one really knew how much such a package ought to cost. Health care reformers in favor of universal access regardless of ability to pay often argued that such cost increases were inevitable and thus acceptable. Almost everyone else argued they were not. It remained a matter for social definition.

Critics of the health care system, which by the early 1970's included almost everyone who did not make a living from it and many who did, focused on and disagreed about many different issues. On two points, however, they spoke with one voice. They believed that the health care system was a mess and that physicians were primarily responsible for it. This newly emergent attitude marked the beginning of the end of a love affair the American public had carried on with the medical profession for over fifty years.

These events occurred during a historical moment when clinical medicine, with a level of technology that sometimes rivaled science fiction, seemed to promise more to the popular imagination than it had ever done. It serviced unprecedented numbers of people. It was seen as a social right of all citizens. Although the health care system was beginning a period of radical transformation, it was in no danger of disappearing as an institution. Why were its power arrangements beginning to undergo a shake-up?

One could more reasonably ask why the American medical profession ever became so powerful in the first place, for physicians are an anomaly in contemporary America, the only occupational group to have gained control not only over the conditions of their own work but over the social institution in which they do it. How were they able to achieve that? An then, having achieved it, why were they beginning to lose control?

Other analysts, particularly Paul Starr, have explained correctly that the medical profession acquired its power over the health care system because that process was congruent with and supported by other important developments within the larger social structure.[2] Some of these supporting components were "cultural," ranging from changes in public attitudes toward occupational licensing to technological developments in communication (the telephone) and transportation (the automobile) that enabled physicians to service larger numbers of people than they could do before, making health care delivery a much more profitable commodity. Other structural supports were "social," involving actions by interest groups. Starr singles out reformers, labor, and insurance companies as groups whose political activities had the unintended consequence of supporting a professional monopoly over health care by physicians.

Correct as this account is, one area to investigate has remained untouched—the role of major American corporations in fostering the professional monopoly. Starr's historical data provides evidence to support speculation that he leaves undone. For example, during the early part of this century, reformers pressed for passage of national health insurance legislation that would have provided compensation for work time lost due to illness. This benefit was considered even more important than payment for health care, which at that time was relatively cheap; if delivered in a hospital ward, it was free. The loss of wages, on the other hand, could and did have tragic consequences. Furthermore, occupational disability and death litigation were perhaps the hottest political issue of the day. During this period employers lobbied frantically for passage of a workers' compensation law that would simultaneously reduce their own liability and remove this issue from public debate. The health insurance proposals put forward by reformers were serious competitive alternatives to the legislation sought by employers.

Support from corporate foundations was an important part of the process through which the American Medical Association (AMA) gained control over medical education during the first two decades of the twentieth century. The Carnegie Foundation funded the famous "Flexner Report" in 1910, thus helping to close down a large number of medical schools that did not meet the kinds of standards the AMA was trying to establish. These schools trained doctors of relatively low social status and produced practitioners in larger numbers than the medical marketplace could support. As a result, the services of physicians were very cheap during that period. The

Rockefeller Foundation provided essential subsidies for the kind of schools favored by the AMA. This assured that medical education and practice would be restricted to a small elite of white, Protestant, upper-class males for the next sixty years, at which time attempts to control soaring health care costs led American industry to try to reverse the professional elitism it had helped to create.

When insurance proposals were first put forward by reformers, the AMA supported them; later it joined the opposition movement represented largely by industry. Thus the prestige of the AMA, established with the aid of foundation subsidies, helped lend respectability to opposition by employers to health insurance that was in competition with their own program of workers' compensation.

In discussing the results of a refined tuberculin test in 1907 that indicated that many people were infected with tuberculosis who were not themselves sick, Starr notes that the AMA opposed a social-reform type of public health measure that would have stressed improvements in nutrition, housing, and working conditions. Such reforms would also have been very expensive for employers; presumably the prospect would have been as repugnant to them as were passage and enforcement of OSHAct regulations to their 1970 counterparts. Furthermore, an open public discussion of this method of dealing with tuberculosis would have added fire to labor's already strident demands for improved wages and working conditions. The AMA promoted a private health care system utilizing curative medicine based on laboratory science. It opposed a "public health" philosophy of health care rooted in notions of social reform. Employers would certainly have shared this AMA philosophy.

It is true, as Starr points out, that the ability of physicians to control legislative decisions in their own interest has been their single most powerful structural support, particularly during the period from the mid–1940's, when health care services began to experience such unprecedented expansion as a result of the growth of labor unions and the emergence of health insurance as a fringe benefit. This influence over legislation helped physicians to avoid becoming organized as a public service agency, a prospect that would certainly have met with opposition from other groups than physicians. One cannot imagine that corporate America wished to see health care services organized under government auspices or even that it would have been indifferent to the prospect.

Legislative power, like professional power, is a social process; it requires social structural support. It is not enough to say that the AMA was a well-oiled lobbying machine, although, of course, it was. One must ask, Of what does lobbying power consist? Totally different images come to mind when we attribute it to, say, corporate America, than to environmental health groups. Or to the AMA. In what did the legislative power of the AMA inhere?

During the same period in which physicians were consolidating control over one single health care system, corporate America was becoming more powerful than many nation-states. Its political and economic power is staggering. Its lobbying apparatus is the best that money and influence can buy. It is quite simply inconceivable that crucial government regulation, which affected not only corporate revenues but the entire economy, could ever have been left to the self-interested whims of one occupational group for such an extended period and with such disastrous results without intervention by corporate America—not unless the interests of that occupational group were somehow compatible with its own. That assumption has to be the bottom line in any theoretical analysis in which power is seen to exist because it is structurally supported, both historically and as an ongoing process. No analysis can either exclude, subordinate, or equate with other relatively weak social components the single most important force within our social structure—American capitalism.

Perhaps the data do not exist that would provide direct evidence that corporate interests were compatible with and contributed in large degree to the emergence of the dominant medical profession during the first two decades of this century. But the processes through which such interests are now facilitating its decline can be documented.

As groundwork for constructing such a case, two points should be stressed. First, all attempts to alter the health care system through government legislation and social policy implementation have failed. Most analysts have attributed that failure to the power of physicians, supported by other interested parties within the health care system, to subvert such attempts. Second, the system developed in the first place as a structural process rather than as the result of deliberate social policy. It follows that to alter such a powerful institution as the American health care system requires not policy planning but strategies through which the structural supports that created and maintained it can be withdrawn. Social forms do not survive because they are functional, but because they are connected. Any significant changes in the health care system would require attacks on the structural supports that facilitated its development historically. In particular, structural supports for professional authority must be eliminated, since that authority is the heart of a traditional, physician-dominated health care system. The specific actions through which such a strategy is expressed must simultaneously create new structural components that would support an alternative health care system with a different authority base.

To manipulate the social structure in this coordinated way would require enormous social, economic, and political power, as well as an intelligent, well-articulated plan. Corporate America has all these things and has been using them strategically since the early 1970's. I do not suggest that a conspiracy exists. On the contrary, those who are engaged in this endeavor intend it to be, among other things, a service to the country. They generously provide information to any interested party who asks. They write extensively about their strategies and tactics. Some of these writings represent an extremely sophisticated understanding of the working of social processes. Industry is using sociological insights to do a very effective kind of policy planning and implementation.

INDUSTRY COMES TO HEALTH CARE

At exactly the moment when the health care system was discovered to be in crisis, industry presented itself as a group that could challenge professional authority. Since the mid–1940's, industry had become a new and powerful health care consumer, buying health care coverage for about forty million Americans. This group is made up of American corporations that have become increasingly activist in the health care arena since the early 1970's. Throughout this book I will refer to it as "industry," which I define in the same way as does a major lobbyist and spokesperson for the group, Willis Goldbeck. Although the term refers to all types of private sector employers, its major reference is to extremely large companies with such enormous power as both purchasers and employers that "their private decisions concerning health care benefits become public decisions affecting the economics of the entire health delivery system."[3]

Like the health care system, industry has been intensely affected by cultural and social events during the last thirty years. Consequently, it has several historically new motives for attempting to exercise control over health care delivery. First, business interests have been alarmed by rapid increases in the amount of the gross national product (GNP) consumed by health care costs. These increases are blamed in large part for inflation throughout the economy; for that reason, industry sees inflation as an indirect cost of health care that it is forced to pay.

Second, because health care has become an important fringe benefit, industry sees itself as paying these rapidly increasing costs directly as well as indirectly. While some consumer groups disagree—arguing that employers pass the cost along, either taking them out of employee wages or raising prices[4]—this is clearly not the perspective of industry.[5]

Third, corporations are increasingly liable for health impairment suffered by employees and sometimes non-employees as a result of federal legislation such as the Coal Mine Health and Safety Act (1969), the Occupational Safety and Health Act (1970), the Rehabilitation Act (1973), and the Toxic Substances Control Act (1976). This liability raises very thorny questions for industry. It involves mass screening of employees exposed to hazardous substances, which could be both expensive and politically dangerous for industry because of the massive extent of unsuspected health problems, work-related and otherwise, that it could uncover.

Fourth, corporations are intent upon collecting and maintaining control over health care data concerning their employees. Such data are required for both "rational" health care planning and policy legitimation. Following a time-honored tradition, industry would like to use only data that support its own positions. Employee health data could be used either to prove or to disprove corporate liability for occupationally induced disabilities or environmental health damages. Collection and control of such a data base have historically been frustrated by numerous laws and rules that are firmly embedded in the professional monopoly over medical practice.

For all these reasons, in the early 1970's business leaders began to form organizations with the expressed purpose of restructuring the health delivery system.[6] The Business Roundtable created its Health Task Force, chaired by Charles J. Pilliod, Jr., Chairman of the Board of Goodyear Tire and Rubber Company.[7]

In 1972 the Conference Board, an independent, non-profit business research organization, convened the first national meeting of
interested parties, including corporate executives, health care
professionals, and representatives of government "to consider ways
in which the business community can improve the delivery of health
care services." Conference participants were advised that "a massive
restructuring of a major industry is . . . taking place. It is an industry whose methods and structures the business community has
both the right and the obligation to study and seek to improve."[8]

The Washington Business Group on Health (WBGH) was established in 1974 at the suggestion of the Business Roundtable; the
WBGH is under the leadership of Willis Goldbeck and is a major
force in corporate health care activism.[9] It began with five companies as members; by 1983 it had almost 200 member companies,
145 of which were major corporations.[10]

The Center for Industry and Health Care (CIHC) was established within the Boston University Health Policy Institute in 1977
by Richard Egdahl, M.D., in conjunction with the WBGH and with
individual corporations.[11] The CIHC provides an academic base and
convenes regular conferences attended by corporate and labor union
leaders, by specialists in the planning, finance, organization, and
evaluation of health care, and by physicians and administrators actually delivering health care in corporate settings.

A number of papers presented at these conferences have been
published as the Springer Series on Industry and Health Care, which
now includes nine volumes.[12] These volumes synthesize conference
discussions, report on special research, and describe health policy
initiatives launched by selected participant corporations. They are
not objective analyses by disinterested researchers but are how-to
accounts by corporate administrators stating what it is they hope to
accomplish and describing the strategies and tactics they have developed in order to reach their goals. These volumes document
strategic and organized intervention in health care planning and policy
making by industry. They are a major data source for this book and
will be referred to in the text hereafter as "the Series." Footnotes
will identify individual books by volume numbers.

Since its inception the CIHC has worked closely with Willis
Goldbeck of the WBGH. Goldbeck wrote the second volume of the
Series himself and was guest editor for the ninth. The seventh vol-

ume consists primarily of papers that were written by industry representatives and delivered at the 1978 annual meeting of the WBGH.

In addition to the Series, various periodicals that are directed toward physicians, hospital administrators, producers, advertisers, purchasers, and consumers of medical products function as data sources. They provide two kinds of supporting documentation. First, they report actions taken by government agencies, corporations, insurers, or consumers that affect the medical marketplace, and they identify the important committees and persons involved. This source provides an indicator of whether, how, and how effectively corporate initiatives listed in the Series are being implemented. Second, they report on economic events in the medical marketplace that point back to corporate initiatives.

A third source of information is provided by various publications by consumer groups, such as Nader's Health Research Group, and reports of government actions and regulations that link to corporate initiatives. For example, a Nader group booklet on radiation exposure supports an early strategy of corporate planners to legitimate the limitation of expensive high-technology diagnostic procedures on the grounds that they are unhealthy.

Industry is, of course, structurally well located to have a major impact on the health care system. It already possesses sophisticated administrative structures, a powerful lobbying apparatus, economic resources, social and economic connections with insurance carriers, captive patient-employees, and a set of health care initiatives that are often congenial with demands of many consumer groups and environmentalists.

The health care system cannot be transformed without also transforming its authority base. The two emerged together as two sides of a coin; neither could exist in its present form without the other. For that reason, only two logical, tactical possibilities exist. Either physicians must be changed into something other than "professionals," or someone other than professionals must become the new authority. Which of these goals orients industry's strategy? The answer is both. Industry wishes both to impose external controls over physicians and to recreate professionalism itself. Both goals may be achieved simultaneously by transforming professionals into bureaucrats.

BUREAUCRAT, M.D.

The bureaucratization process has been so typical of contemporary developments that, at least until the 1970's, a major part of the literature of medical sociology was directed toward attempts to explain how physicians had managed to avoid it. Industry aims to correct that situation and "rationalize" the health care system in keeping with precepts that have proved profitable in business. The manipulation of bureaucratization processes is an important part of its intervention strategy. The ways in which those processes function are described throughout this book.

Sociologists often analyze bureaucracy and professionalism not only as alternative principles for organizing and controlling work but as antithetical principles for legitimating occupational authority.[14] Historically, both bureaucracy and professionalism emerged as part of other long-range processes, including (1) the historical transfer of rights and obligations from the private to the public sphere as part of the creation of social services; (2) the elaboration of a congruent "professional" ideology of work, along with the development of a belief in "social rights" and in the superiority of social as opposed to personal solutions to problems; (3) the emergence and growth of both public and private organizations to fill these new social functions; (4) the increasingly large, complex, specialized, and interdependent character of social institutions; and (5) the development of administrative and scientific technologies, along with the economically and politically interested occupational specialties required to staff them.

These developments and many others contributed to the emergence of both bureaucracy and professionalism as ways to organize, control, and legitimate both authority and employment monopolies. These developments were, of course, both cultural and social, but our major interest lies in their social determinants.

Industry's strategy of using bureaucratic organization to defeat rivals for power has venerable historical precedents. For example, in the feudal era the interest of the secular ruler lay in giving out jobs on the basis of bureaucratic principles, such as appropriate training and subordination to hierarchical authority, rather than according to birth. This practice simultaneously made administration more flexible and served to reduce the power of those who had appropriated traditional rights, the patrimonial lords. This form of work allocation thus facilitated the development of both a secular state and bureaucratic administration and contributed to the decline of traditional power arrangements.[15]

The development of medicine in medieval Europe provides another example. With the support of the major social institutions of the time—Church, University, and State—physicians achieved an occupational monopoly during a historical moment when medical technology was empirically inferior to that of the "witches" they replaced.[16] Weber describes this process of professionalization as one in which a status group becomes embedded in an "overarching communal network," through which it is able to mobilize social power to create and maintain occupational monopolies.[17]

In these two examples, neither bureaucratic nor professional authority developed because of its own intrinsic merits; rather, they were structurally supported.

Regardless of the conditions of their emergence, bureaucracy and professionalism are two of the most important social developments of modern times. They represent the major processes through which authority is legitimated in the industrialized world. For that reason, and because bureaucratization is a major component of industry's strategy to transform health care delivery, I will differentiate between the legitimating bases of "professional" and "bureaucratic" authority for the purposes to which these distinctions will be put in this analysis.

Formally, both bureaucracy and professionalism are legitimated by claims of some kind of tested or certified competence or knowledge. Both claim to be rational. The nature of that rationality is often problematic because the term itself is ambiguous. It is commonly used to refer both to systematic methodologies, which are neutral and automatic, and to cognitive processes associated with cause-effect relationships. Both bureaucratic and professional authority claim to be based on cognitive as well as systematic rationality. However, bureaucratic tasks often utilize predominantly systematic methodologies because their goal is usually to coordinate many different parts efficiently. For professionals who are physicians, rationality usually refers to the cause-effect relationships between their treatment of one, or one category of, client and its outcome. In both cases, the kind of rationality valued is the kind that will do the job at hand.

Both groups legitimate their occupational authority by claiming to make decisions on the basis of these problematic rational considerations. The physician, ideally, makes rational decisions because they result in improved health and are thus in the interest of both client and society. According to this model, the physician is motivated to put those interests before his of her own by a "service ethic," which is considered to be so highly valued, ingrained, and sanctioned that it is peculiar to this occupational category. Pressure from peers is expected to provide the only enforcement necessary to ensure that decisions are actually made on the basis of this superior ethic.

The bureaucrat, ideally, makes rational decisions because they are most efficient in meeting the goals of the organization. The bureaucrat is supposed to be motivated to put these goals before personal ones because mechanisms that are part of the organizational structure make him or her accountable to a superior on the hierarchical ladder. Much of the work done within bureaucratic organizations consists of processes through which individuals can account to each other for the work they say they are doing.

The issue of trust is, of course, crucial to both groups. It is often said that the authority of physicians cannot function without trust and that this is a trouble because, of course, trust is always open to abuse. Physicians may make self-interested decisions and then exploit public trust as a purely ritualistic legitimator of their actions. Of course, such a process does violence to society because it undermines the notion of trust itself, sometimes eliminating it for a time as a human value, capacity, or legitimating mechanism.

The accountability of the bureaucrat is also open to abuse, because it often means only that the person who made the decision was legally entitled to have made it, not that it was made on a rational basis. Accountability can also be used to conceal or rationalize rather than prevent self-interested decisions. Perhaps most significantly, the concept of accountability as a legitimating mechanism also does violence to society, in that it institutionalizes distrust as a normal part of its routine functioning, suggesting as it does that people will do what they claim to be doing only if they are watched.

BUREAUCRATIC V. PROFESSIONAL GOALS AND RATIONALITY

Contemporary developments have been toward the increased polarization of professional and bureaucratic authority principles. Both the technological and organizational spheres have emerged separately as monolithic, power-claiming fields in the modern world. But the bases of their respective claims to rationality have become increasingly problematic. Since rationality can be justified in terms of both goals and methods, it is true that administration as well as science may be called rational. But because the types of rationality involved require different kinds of training and are based on different ultimate goals, they may actually be in conflict. A simple example will illustrate this point.[18]

The New York City Health Department provides various services to children in the public schools, such as vaccines and physicians to administer them. In 1971 the board of governors of a union representing Health Department physicians complained to the office of the commissioner of health, also a physician, that school health rooms had no refrigerators and that, consequently, the vaccines were unrefrigerated. The president of the physicians' union threatened a job action if the situation was not corrected. After a number of discussions between union and Health Department officials, the union was persuaded to accept the situation even though, as one board member put it, "worthless vaccines are sometimes injected into children."

In this case, Health Department administrator-physicians had at least two different goals; one was to maintain the health of school children with currently available technological procedures, and the other was to coordinate the treatment of children with available supplies and physicians. The goals were different and may or may not have been in conflict, depending, in this case, on the condition of the unrefrigerated vaccines, determined in part by such extraneous factors as the season of the year, and on the effect they had on children. If there was a conflict, it remained invisible. Although all decisions were made by people who were technical experts by training, the decision that was finally reached was not based on principles of technical expertise. The doctors gave up the battle when they were told that electricity and refrigerators would be turned off in the schools during non-school hours. Within complex organizations there are no provisions for dealing with uncategorized elements such as a single refrigerator humming in a darkened building.

There are differences and possible conflicts between the goals and methods of technological as opposed to purely administrative decision making. Disputes may arise from opinions about which technical experts themselves disagree, of course; in such a case the limits of technological knowledge and of expertise are apparent. But in organizations where professionals and bureaucrats work together with parallel lines of authority, conflict can be expected to arise because the best, or sometimes only, defensible decision that can be made, such as to refrigerate vaccines, falls on the wrong side of an "efficiency-effectiveness" ratio that is determined by administrators.

Although it seems reasonable to expect conflict over such issues, the fact is that it rarely occurs. Parsons believed this to be true because when physicians work in organizational settings, they lose only "administrative," not "technical," freedom.[19] Goss attributes this equilibrium to the development of "parallel authority systems" between physicians and administrators.[20]

When physicians lose authority, however, it is as likely to be in technological and scientific areas as in administrative ones. In fact, it is specifically in treatment and diagnostic decisions that industry intends to effect changes in physicians' behavior, because this is seen as the only possible way to cut health care costs. The changes are to be brought about by imposing bureaucratic accountability on professional decision making. Of course, individual professionals may make "bad" medical decisions in the process of doing their work. The entire profession may do so when an erroneous belief gains general acceptance. Within bureaucratic settings, however, such decisions may be not random, accidental, nor idiosyncratic, but may be systematized, routinized, and universally applied on the basis of cost-efficiency. For example, in the case of the school health physicians the decision was consciously made to administer unrefrigerated vaccines as a matter of routine, everyday practice. While it may be the case that individual physicians in private practice fail to keep refrigerators in their offices or to refrigerate materials that require it, one would not expect such a practice to be routinized and universal.

PROFESSIONAL LEGITIMATIONS, BUREAUCRATIC DECISIONS

Modern bureaucracy utilizes the major legitimating devices of professional authority—that is, education and training—to secure the monopolization of the right to do certain kinds of work. Such monopolies require support from the societies or institutions in which they exist. The support may vary from outright legal prohibition of competition, which is enjoyed by physicians, lawyers, and architects, but not college professors, to a strong grant of public trust. In the past, bureaucratic administrators have not had either of these kinds of support. The "legal" component of the bureaucrat's "technical-legal authority" refers only to the rights and obligations that bureaucrats enjoy as they are defined by job descriptions within specific organizations. Outside the organization, no rights exist. A person could not be arrested for practicing administration without a license. An administrator, when separated from a job, is an unemployed person. A doctor is a doctor is a doctor.

Even if administrators have received scientific-technical training, they cannot make administrative decisions purely on the basis of that training. In this situation, when professionals and bureaucrats work together, professional expertise may function to legitimate bureaucratic authority without being the basis for decisions that are actually made. For example, peer standards review organizations (PSROs, discussed in chapter 2) have been used by corporate administrators and government agencies to force changes in physician practices that were determined by the administrators, even though the PSROs are run by physicians.

To the extent that this is a general pattern, it means that technical expertise may function to legitimate bureaucratic authority, but not to guarantee that the most rational technical or scientific decisions will be made. The same may be true for physicians (those who administer unnecessary treatments to patients, for example), but such practices are considered reprehensible, even when they are widespread. They do not thus become "routinized," that is, consciously systematized and publicly universal. They are not legitimated by a bottom-line philosophy, as bureaucratic decisions often are. For example, 33 percent of hysterectomies have been estimated to be unnecessary.[21] The facts that feminist groups have criticized surgeons severely and that third-party payers have attempted to control the number of hysterectomies performed are indicators that the practice is considered reprehensible and is thought to be widespread. However, the largest single group to have such surgeries is doctors' wives; presumably physicians actually believe in the efficacy of this surgery. To diminish its incidence, therefore, requires that they redefine reality. This is exactly what began to happen when the second-opinion process put pressure on physicians to do fewer hysterectomies. The bottom-line philosophy, on the other hand, does not require that anyone be self-deluded. If renal dialysis is defined as not cost-efficient, many would agree with President Reagan that it is acceptable to implement policies that would limit it, even though the procedure is required to sustain life. Strength and courage are required not by the patient but by the policy maker, who must bite the bullet and make the rational (cost-efficient) decision.

INDUSTRY'S STRATEGY FOR CHANGE

Industry's earliest attempts to exercise control over the health care system were relatively unorganized and involved mainly the promotion of health maintenance organizations (HMOs). These events will be described in chapter 4. Within a very short time it was recognized that these efforts would not do the job. Industry, exemplified by Goodyear Tire and Rubber, then began to develop what the Council of Wage and Price Stability described as a "holistic" (sic) approach.

It is holistic in a double sense. First, the company is involved in every aspect of controlling costs—the costs of benefits administration, of unwarranted individual claims, of systemwide patterns of inappropriate utilization, and of building health care facilities. Second, Goodyear focuses on the system, not particular practitioners, hospitals, or medical procedures. The company's emphasis is on altering general patterns of health care delivery rather than reducing individual claims that may not be fully warranted.[22]

The "systemic" approach attempts to influence every part of the system at once, rather than just one aspect of it or providers themselves, in order to bring about change. In this theoretical approach, providers are expected to change their behavior in response to changes in their environments, both in their immediate work settings and in the larger world. Therefore, advocates of the systemic approach try to effect both. The ways in which this is done are described throughout this book. They include support for certain kinds of government regulations, such as those that established peer standards review organizations (chapter 2) and health systems agencies (chapter 5), both of which were bitterly opposed by health care providers; direct involvement whenever possible by corporate representatives in health care planning, especially for expenditures for construction of capital equipment; manipulation of third-party reimbursement policies to encourage or discourage certain kinds of utilization; education of employee-patients to encourage them to criticize and challenge providers; and many others.

Industry uses whatever data and arguments are available to undertake its initiatives to restructure the health care system; it uses theory and research from both radical and conservative groups to make its own points, with absolute pragmatism. Thus it is able to argue simultaneously that soaring health care costs are the result of government regulations such as Medicare and Medicaid, which expanded access to previously underserved groups; economic incentives that reward providers for delivering unnecessary services; hypochondriacal people who live infantile lifestyles; treatments that may be necessary to sustain life, but only for a few, and that therefore are not cost-efficient; and the professional "guild" or"cartel," which prevents the operation of free market mechanisms. The contradictory features of these arguments form a disorienting fabric of background assumptions that are never questioned in industry's analyses.

Industry's theorizing is an important component of its intervention strategy; it serves as an ideology to stimulate action. Two underlying beliefs are expressed throughout the Series. First, the private sector, led by industry, can restructure and run the health care system "better" than government or providers. This, according to Pilliod of Goodyear, is because the government has a bad record in the area of efficiency.[23] Clearly it is not only physicians who oppose government control.

Second, running the system "better" means running it more "cost-efficiently." As Kaplan of United States Administrators says: "We've been able to prove that cost containment and quality of care go hand in hand. When you discover doctors overutilizing and cut down on that, you improve the quality of care."[24]

Kaplan and his firm will be discussed in chapter 3. They represent the most radical early attempts to standardize and rationalize medical delivery under the administrative control of third-party payers that I encountered. Although quality of care is an often mentioned topic for Kaplan, it is clear that the quality sought is always cost control.

According to both the Series and the provider press, consumer activities have increased over the last decade, especially since corporations are now defined as consumers of primary importance. That fact has had an effect on the health care sector, as indicated by this 1979 editorial in *Modern Healthcare*.

Major employers, insurers and third-party payers are moving strongly against soaring healthcare costs and in many areas they are reducing hospital occupancy. . . . Central Illinois hospitals and those near other plants of Caterpillar Tractor Co., and Deere and Co. are feeling the effect of utilization reviews by professional standards review organizations hired by the firms to reduce their employees' hospital stays. . . . Other companies and insurers are also hiring PSROs, which the medical establishment has tried to pass off as being ineffective. . . . What this means is that the free markets are working. The health care industry is finally running into strong consumer resistance to soaring prices and expenditures. This free market competition is coming not from other healthcare providers but from suppliers of other goods and services. . . . Employers and insurers . . . are acting as agents for the prospective patients, giving them clout they've never had before.[25]

This definition of corporations as consumers is very important. Industry's insistence on that status is politically motivated. The National Health Planning and Resources Development Act of 1974 (P.L. 93–641) mandated consumer majorities on health systems agencies, which industry saw as important structural mechanisms through which it might implement its initiatives. Thus, its consumer status legitimates participation on planning boards, where industry feels it is uniquely qualified to serve. Industry defines itself as the rational consumer. Whereas the medical system, patients, government, and insurers have failed to assume responsibility for costs and have passed those costs down the line from one to the other, business has no incentive for such behavior. It sees itself as paying those costs (as opposed to the view of consumer groups and labor, who believe *they* pay the costs, in the form of higher prices and reduced wages) rather than passing them on to others. This, presumably, motivates industry to be truly responsible in its planning and in the setting of initiatives.

REDEFINING HEALTH CARE DELIVERY
REALITY

Just at the moment that health care services were socially acknowledged as a right of all citizens, health care technology had begun to accomplish unprecedented wonders. One of industry's major criticisms of the health care system is that this high-technology
medicine is not cost-efficient. "High-technology medicine" is a term
industry uses to refer to a wide range of processes. It may refer to
utilization of sophisticated equipment such as a CT scanner or to
mundane chest X-rays. It may mean gadgetry of questionable value
or clearly useful devices that are not cost-efficient because they serve
only one category of patient.

Industry attacks high-technology medicine on two major counts.
First, it does not work. For example, Goldbeck tells us that "people
are now beginning to question the appropriateness of intensive
care. . . . A few studies have shown that cardiac patients and ac-
cident victims appear to do at least as well, and in some cases better, when treated at home."[26]

Of course when overutilization of health care services first became a major social topic, critics of the system defined it simply as
the unnecessary hospitalization of people who were not seriously
ill; such services should be restricted to those whose conditions
warranted them. Now we are told that overutilization means hos-
pitalizing serious cases as well.

Second, industry maintains that high-technology medicine may
actually be harmful. In this context, the Series often quotes statements made by radical women's groups about overutilization of
hysterectomies and generalizes from that data to other kinds of surgeries for which no evidence of overutilization is adduced.

Third, even effective technology may be cost-ineffective because
it is useful to just one category of patient, as opposed to the population as a whole. The Series states, "Some of these products will
be cost-ineffective if you look at just one life versus many. Industry
ought to get together and make some value judgements, just as it
does on national health insurance and HMOs."[27]

Examples of these products include the beta cell, renal dialysis,
and transplants. Such products "cost a lot and huge numbers of
people will want them."[28] Clearly it is not just unnecessary services

but high technology providing life-and-death functions that industry opposes. It uses the language of consumerism; renal dialysis is referred to as something huge numbers of people will "want," not as a procedure necessary to sustain life. The desire is clearly to eliminate third-party reimbursement for such procedures in the future. They are not cost-efficient because they are only useful for "one category of patient."

Industry attempts to foster the idea that health care services should be democratically distributed, rather than provided on the basis of the patient's condition. This view is now reflected in some studies of the health care system that have been reported by the media. For example, in May 1980 the *New York Times* reported that two different studies had identified "high-cost" patients:

The findings of two new studies have shed light on who puts the heaviest burden on America's health care system, an important factor in establishing any economically feasible plan for national health insurance. . . . A survey of the records of 2,238 patients in six hospitals, mostly in Boston, concluded that a mere 13 percent of the patients used as much medical and hospital services as the remaining 87 percent. If that reflects the national picture, then only 1.3 percent of the population consumes more than half the hospital resources.[29]

Christopher J. Zook, co-author of the study, said, "We spend a lot of time worrying about cost control for low-cost people," and added that "perhaps more attention should be focused on the small number who devour most of the hospital resources."

Although it does not appear remarkable that the segment of the population that is most seriously ill receives most of the health care services, the *Times* expressed the belief that this finding should influence any "catastrophic coverage" provision included in the national health insurance plans being considered at that time: "The disproportionate use of hospital services by a small group may hold lessons for the framers of national health insurance. The catastrophic coverage embodied in President Carter's version would be subject to a $2,500 deductible."[30] Clearly such a deductible would have been intended to discourage utilization of crucially required care.

Industry displays some ambivalence about limiting technological development of medical care products. No one would advocate withholding renal dialysis or heart implants from those who can pay for them. Furthermore, the development of such products represents profits for industry. As the Series says, "The private sector, with much money involved in prototype development and possible future sales and yet so much other money in employee health benefits packages, may want to express an informed viewpoint on new technology and technological assessment."[31]

THE TRANSFORMATION OF HEALTH CARE GOALS

When industry first began its intervention attempts in the early 1970's, cost-efficiency was not perceived as a legitimate goal of the health care system. The Series never advocated cuts in necessary services; its major thrust was to define a significant percentage of diagnostic and treatment procedures delivered or prescribed by physicians as "overutilization" and to eliminate only that. At that time, no political or public support could have been found for the argument that necessary services should be withheld because they were not cost-efficient. And industry's planners understood the political danger in withdrawing health care benefits once they had been given and defined as a right. It is also possible that industry believed its "unnecessary utilization" argument was correct. However, after more than ten years of attempts to cut costs by ferreting out these procedures, costs in the health care sector continue to rise. In 1983 the Reagan administration mandated a new fixed-payment system of billing, called "diagnosis related groups," for Medicaid and Medicare patients. This system is discussed in chapter 2. It represents the biggest change in Medicaid and Medicare since their enactment in the mid–1960's and will certainly result in cuts in medical services to the poor and elderly.[32] Such cuts would be accomplished not by changing the law, but through the implementation of a "rational" payment formula. Also in 1983, major corporations began to withdraw health benefits won by labor unions through collective bargaining without repercussions from workers, who were fearful of losing their jobs.[33] There is no longer any need to argue that health care services are unnecessary to justify eliminating them. It is enough that they cost "too much."

These changes may well by supported by popular opinion, not only because cutting health care costs has become a legitimate and widely accepted goal but also because attitudes about health and health services delivery have changed. All over the country "alternative" treatment modalities are springing up—"surgicenters," which receive third-party reimbursement, and "emergicenters," which are striving for that kind of recognition. And patients are increasingly seeking other sources of treatment than M.D.s., the provider press reports.[34] This is a very different mood from the rather extraordinary public confidence that hospitals and physicians have enjoyed until very recently. There is a new public faith in self-help, similar to the tone of the popular health movements of the mid-nineteenth century, which disdained elite professionalism.

In some ways we seem to have come full circle, back to the mood of the late nineteenth century, when many different treatment styles were widely accepted. This was precisely the fragmentation of the profession that the AMA eliminated during the first two decades of this century, with the help of corporate foundations and the Flexner Commission.

The significance of this mood must not be overstated, of course. Those with serious medical problems do not generally choose either the self-help option or the services of paraprofessionals if they can negotiate the price of high-technology medical care. But it is one indication of the extent to which public perception of health and medical care issues has changed since the late 1960's.

This book is one account of how all these changes have come about.

2

Reimbursement Policies of Third-Party Payers

The emergence of third-party payment plans has been the most crucial development within the health care system during this century. Through these plans the first necessary condition for the delivery of health care services to a mass market was met: a reliable, predictable source of large amounts of cash to pay for it. Thirty years after health care insurance came into existence, health care delivery had become the third largest industry in the United States, following only construction and food. The services of the health care system, like the products of the construction and food industries, had come to be utilized by mass markets and defined as a social right.

Historically, health care providers opposed the development of third-party payment plans because they recognized them as threats to professional autonomy. Providers were forced to abandon this opposition during the depression of the 1930's. Although physicians had firmly established their professional status by that time, their fees were seriously threatened by the fact that people could not afford them. Hospitals were even harder hit; many were forced out of business during this depression, as an unemployed populace returned to the practice of caring for their sick at home.

Once economic conditions pressed for the development of third-party payments, providers used their dominant position in health care delivery to construct a payment system under their own control. In the early 1930's the American Hospital Association (AHA) began to lobby for the enabling legislation that created Blue Cross. Although the American Medical Association fought the process bitterly, less than a decade later the medical societies played a similar role in the development of Blue Shield. From their inception, Blue Cross and Blue Shield were provider controlled and have remained so until recently.

Few would have challenged the legitimacy of physician dominance during that period. But, more importantly, there were no structural elements through which opposition could have been mounted had it existed. Government programs involving health care were minimal and in their embryonic stages. No mass market existed that could have generated a consumer movement. And no collective bargaining or group health care contracts had transformed industry into a powerful customer for health care delivery services.

Once they emerged, third-party payment systems were a potent contributor to the creation of the complex, powerful health care empire described first by the Ehrenreichs and, most recently, by Starr.[1]

Industry recognizes that the third-party reimbursement system has provided a crucial structural support for the development and the continuing existence of the current physician-dominated health delivery system and that it has contributed enormously to health care inflation in the process. The Series identifies four reasons that both private and public insurance plans have had these effects.

First, third-party payments extended access to professional health care services to masses of people who had previously had little or no contact with them. Expansion of the health care delivery system itself became both inevitable and necessary to meet the new demand. Neither private nor public insurance schemes included mechanisms for containing this extraordinary growth, controlling health care resources, or supervising professional personnel. Third-party agents paid whatever charges were made without questioning them. For the last ten years corporate planners have been putting pressure on both public and private insurance plans to implement various techniques for rationing services, including the restructuring of reimbursement policies and the implementing of procedures to define and prevent the overutilization of health care facilities and services. Peer review is the key element in this process.

Second, the extension of insurance coverage for basic health services to large groups of people contributed to the further development of the idea that health care is a right, and it increased the dependence of individuals on professional solutions to health care problems. Corporate planners have initiated programs to induce individuals to take more personal responsibility for their own good health by improving their lifestyles and to make them critical of the overuse of professional services. The programs include both attempts to educate employees and the public and outright payments to people who reduce their utilization rates.

Third, because people who actually used health care did not pay for it themselves, neither they nor their providers were motivated to take costs into account when making diagnostic and treatment decisions. The erroneous idea developed that "more is better"; this not only contributed enormously to runaway costs but also exposed patients to sometimes harmful treatment and diagnostic procedures by utilizing them unnecessarily. Industry supports mechanisms for sharing costs, such as co-insurance and deductibles, both to make patients and providers more aware of the real costs of health care services and to encourage patients to resist undergoing unnecessary procedures.

Fourth, in the past certain third-party reimbursement policies, such as paying for diagnostic and treatment procedures only when they are performed in a hospital, have been conducive to creating excess facilities and beds and to keeping them filled unnecessarily. Corporate planners have successfully pressured insurance carriers to reimburse for procedures performed on an out-patient basis and in alternative treatment facilities, thus helping to stimulate the development of these new forms of delivery.

True to the logic of its own intervention strategy, industry recognizes that the third-party payment system, which helps to create and recreate the current health care system, must itself be restructured. In the beginning, industry was mainly interested in the insurance plans that covered its own employees, although it directed the criticisms listed above at both private and public payment plans. In theory, industry supports publicly funded health care for the poor and the elderly. In practice, it speaks constantly of rationing and eliminating these services, arguing that health care is the right only of those who can pay for it. The role that industry has played in the development of commercial insurance plans suggests that its theoretic support for the concept of publicly funded care is motivated by a wish to maintain the separation between publicly and privately funded populations in order to avoid paying for coverage for anyone except its own employees.

WHO PAYS, WHO BENEFITS

Blue Cross was the first hospital insurance plan in this country.[2] The enabling act that created it was adopted by the New York State Legislature in 1934; by 1945, similar laws had been adopted in thirty-five states.

State and federal enabling legislation provided Blue Cross with special corporate status as a charitable and benevolent organization and exempted it both from maintaining reserves, which are required of commercial insurers, and from paying federal taxes. Almost half the states with enabling legislation also exempt the plans from state taxes.

Blue Cross received this favored status initially because it provided a community service; it offered hospital insurance to everyone at the same rate, its community rating. Because Blue Cross averaged out the cost to the entire community, this method was beneficial to the poor, unemployed, and elderly, who utilized more services than young, employed people. Commercial companies, unencumbered by legislation, were able to give lower rates to groups that utilized fewer services, called experience rating. Of course it was recognized that if the healthiest component pulled out of the community pool, community rating would become prohibitively expensive. Favored status was intended to protect Blue Cross from this commercial competition.

The insurance industry developed rapidly during and after World War II, right along with labor unions. As employment rates and wages rose, health coverage became an increasingly important item in collective bargaining, offering something for everyone. It provided tax benefits for employers, who could write off payments of fringe benefits, and for employees, who received a non-taxable service cheaper than they could buy it individually out of taxable income. In both cases the government helped subsidize industry's fringe benefit of health insurance for employed people by forgoing taxes, a politically popular move both then and now. (A proposal by the

Reagan administration to eliminate this tax benefit on the grounds that it would help control health care inflation by "discouraging the purchase of extensive amounts of health insurance" provoked opposition from some very diverse groups. These included the Chamber of Commerce of the United States, the National Association of Manufacturers, the American Federation of Labor and Congress of Industrial Organizations, half a dozen affiliated unions, the National Council of Senior Citizens, Blue Cross and Blue Shield, and many commercial insurance companies.)[3]

Both Blue Cross and commercial insurers flourished during this time. But in spite of its favored status, Blue Cross suffered from commercial competition. In 1945 it had 61 percent of the hospital insurance market while commercial carriers had 33 percent; by 1951, commercial carriers had the majority of the market. In the mid–1960's, passage of Medicare and Medicaid divided the insurance market into public and private spheres. By the end of 1969, Blue Cross had 37 percent and commercial carriers 57 percent of the private market although no single one of them was as powerful as the giant "Blues." Commercial insurance carriers, unencumbered by community service requirements, could offer coverage at lower rates. Corporations negotiating group insurance coverage for their employees increasingly chose to offer commercial carriers in order to avoid partially subsidizing care for the poor, elderly, and unemployed. Further governmental aid, administration of Medicare and Medicaid, helped Blue Cross to survive this competition.

Industry blames third-party payment systems, public and private, for most of the economic problems of the health care system on the grounds that they all catered to and supported inefficiency and overutilization by providers. However, it was clearly the emergence of corporations as powerful consumers of health care that supported the development of health insurance as a major industry in the first place. Even more importantly, industry's creaming-off of experience-rated plans for the elite of the insured population resulted in the creation of two-class health coverage just at a historical moment when the ideology of health care as a right was emerging. This made the future development of such programs as Medicare and Medicaid virtually inevitable.

It is partly because industry is aware of the role it has played in these historical developments that its planners decided they could use insurance carriers to force changes in the system. Industry's power as a large-scale consumer of group health plans provided a structural support for the development of the health care insurance industry. That support can now be either manipulated or withdrawn as a tactic to weaken the historic bond between providers and insurance carriers, especially the most powerful single carrier, Blue Cross and Blue Shield, in an effort to restructure third-party reimbursement policies.

CUTTING THE CORD

In the late 1970's industry provided strong and historically uncharacteristic support for government anti-trust legislation designed to weaken the close relationship between providers and Blue Cross and Blue Shield. In April 1979 the Federal Trade Commission issued a report charging that medical societies and physicians dominate Blue Shield plans, through both ownership and service on their boards, thus prohibiting competition in the health care sector.[4] That year the State of Ohio won an anti-trust suit against the Ohio State Medical Association, which had owned the state's largest Blue Shield organization, Ohio Medical Indemnities, for thirty years.[5] The medical society was ordered to sell its stock back to Ohio Blue Shield for the same amount it had paid for it originally, $56,000. In addition, it was ordered to make a $1 million grant to the state's seven medical schools.

The Federal Trade Commission also charged that hospitals dominate Blue Cross boards in the same way.[6] All this is hardly news. The point is that as a result of anti-trust activities, which were supported by industry, professional control over one of its most crucial structural supports has been publicly labeled illegal.

As a result of these and other, earlier pressures, Blue Cross and Blue Shield began to adopt reimbursement initiatives originally demanded by industry in the early 1970's. Second opinions for surgical procedures are a famous example. In Michigan, pressure from the automotive industry led to a number of the earliest innovations by Blue Cross and Blue Shield, including the following: a prospective rather than a retrospective reimbursement and hospital admissions program. That means costs must be specified in advance and non-emergency hospital admissions approved in advance. Prospective review was extremely repugnant to physicians, but is extraordinarily effective in rationalizing health care. It is the heart of the diagnostic related groups (DRGs) discussed below; a screening procedure designed to restrain escalation in physicians' fees; restriction of out-patient service coverage so it applies only to life-threatening emergencies; and the elimination of reimbursements for routine admission tests.

The provider press has followed these changes in reimbursement policies closely. By 1979 its coverage indicated that Blue Cross and Blue Shield were forming a new alliance with "customers" and were weakening their bond with providers: "The strain in the relationship between the Blues and providers of service is increased by the insurers' move to customer-controlled boards. The Blues are becoming more sensitive to the customers who pay the premium bill and are disengaging from hospitals and other providers of services."[7]

The restructuring of reimbursement policies has always been seen by industry as a major way to make fast cuts in health care costs. However, the Series reflects an increasingly sophisticated understanding of the many ways in which manipulation of the third-party payment system could be used not only to cut immediate costs but to effect profound changes in the health care system. As industry increased its influence over reimbursement policies, it found ways those policies could be extended to support other initiatives. New institutional structures emerged as part of the process. For example, the refusal of carriers to reimburse for non-emergency services or for unnecessary hospital stays required that some formal apparatus be established to determine whether an emergency existed or hospitalization was necessary. Because of the legal monopoly physicians enjoy over medical practice, neither industry nor insurers could tell them directly what and how health care could be delivered. A formal structure was required through which some physicians could tell others what industry wanted to be done and could legitimate the new reimbursement policies being implemented by insurers. Industry found that the basis for such a structure already existed, the historically ineffectual peer and utilization review provisions included in the Medicare and Medicaid legislation of 1964.

THE ORIGINS OF PEER AND UTILIZATION
REVIEW

The passage of Medicare and Medicaid represented the culmination of the ideology that health care is a right. It was a keystone of the Great Society programs, which passed over the opposition of both industry and the AMA during the 1960's. The peer and utilization review provisions contained within this legislation were entirely formalistic. Although they mandated the establishment of a national medical review committee to study utilization patterns and make recommendations for changes, as well as to administer the program, they also specified that the majority of the nine-member committee be physicians, who were not to be supervised or controlled by any federal office or employee.[8] The provisions were worded to protect the autonomy of professionals, whose cooperation was an absolute political requisite for either passage or implementation of Medicare and Medicaid legislation at that time.

The national peer review committee was never even set up by HEW; it simply was not possible to make judgements about either the necessity for or the quality of services without supporting data, which were unavailable. Health care data did exist, of course, but it was useless as the basis for any kind of utilization "policy" function because: (1) it had been collected by the physicians to be reviewed and could not be expected to substantiate "bad" practices; (2) it was in the possession of providers, who did not wish to relinquish it; and (3) it was not centralized, standardized, or otherwise organized in such a way as to establish unambiguous, legitimate standards to which reviewers could enforce universal compliance.

In short, although the formal legislative mandate was available to legitimate peer and utilization review, neither the political climate nor the structural apparatus existed that could have supported such a process. Without utilization review, decisions about the approval of claims were entirely in the hands of insurance carriers who, at that time, were provider dominated.

Passage of Medicare and Medicaid made inevitable a massive influx of new patients into the health care system. That fact alone goes far to explain the severe inflation of health care costs that began almost as soon as the legislation was passed. Medicare and Medicaid mill scandals began to hit the press almost immediately. Inflation, provider abuse, and a growing concern about the costs of the Great Society program in general soon led to legislation directed at control of health care costs. In 1967 Congress passed P.L. 90–248, which made the cost containment goals of peer review very explicit. It stated that regulations would provide safeguards against unnecessary utilization and maintain payments only when charges were reasonable.[9]

The cost of these programs continued to rise alarmingly. Although in 1965 the Senate Finance Committee estimated that Medicare costs for 1970 would be $3.1 billion, the cost was closer to $6 billion. Control over utilization continued to be a major issue. At its 1972 hearings the Senate Finance Committee heard expert testimony that "a significant proportion of the health services provided under Medicare and Medicaid were probably not medically necessary."[10]

Finally, in an attempt to make peer and utilization review work, the 1972 Congress passed P.L. 92–603, the Social Security amendment that created the peer standards review organization (PSRO). This law took review out of the hands of review committees and gave it to local review organizations, which were composed of physicians and osteopaths. The process was still to be physician controlled, but a significant new structural element had been added. The law created a very complex bureaucratic apparatus; 203 areas throughout the country were designated to create review organizations to ensure that health care that was paid for by federal funding—Medicare, Medicaid, and the maternal and child health program—was medically necessary, met professionally recognized standards, and was provided in the least expensive delivery settings available.[11] The amendment required the area PSROs to delegate review responsibility back to those hospitals that were themselves capable of doing effective review.

In 1977 HEW produced a status report indicating that the PSRO was not cost-effective; it did not recover the cost of its own operation.[12] Even worse than its utilization and cost control failures, according to this HEW report, costs might actually rise if PSRO's quality controls were effectively met. The report blamed PSRO ineffectiveness on the fact that it concentrated all its cost containment strategy on overutilization, which had come to represent only a secondary influence on the rate of hospital spending in recent years.

To effectively cut costs, the report declared, many other factors would have to be controlled, factors over which PSRO had no legislative authority, including the prices of materials and wages; the increasingly technological complexity of health care delivery; the demographics of third-party coverage; reimbursement patterns and controls; and the size, distribution, and general health of the population.

Since cost control was the major goal of the legislation, the survival and indeed the growth of the PSRO concept during this period require some explanation.

INDUSTRY'S ROLE IN DEVELOPING PEER REVIEW

In April 1977, three months after the HEW report, Willis Goldbeck told HEW Secretary Califano that, although the program had been less effective than anticipated, the concept was still valid.[13] He predicted that during the next year more employers would try to extend PSRO to the private sector.

Of course PSROs were created by government to regulate *federally* funded health care delivery. Once the structures were created, however, they were available for co-optation by industry to function in the private sector. From industry's point of view, whether or not PSRO met its manifest function was far less important than the many other informal and unstated purposes it served.

Industrial firms have provided economic support for PSRO since its inception. Goodyear funded programs in Akron, Ohio, and in Freeport, Illinois.[14] Deere and Company gave a grant to Iowa State Medical Foundation to help establish PSRO's ability to perform peer and utilization review on private patients. There was a provision in Deere's contract with the United Auto Workers that allowed the company to cease reimbursement within twenty-four hours of PSRO utilization review determination that medical service was no longer required.[15] Ford Motor Company, in combination with General Motors and Chrysler, cites utilization review among its major projects and objectives.[16] Procter and Gamble worked with a Cincinnati foundation that employs full-time nurses to conduct in-hospital reviews of admissions, lengths of stay, and discharges.[17]

With this encouraging support from industry, HEW began to put

real pressure on PSRO to do its job. In April 1979 it denied funding to a PSRO for the first time because of its poor performance.[18]
By August of the same year there were 190 PSROs operating within
the 203 designated areas; at that point, HEW stated there were "just
too many of them" and began to reduce their numbers, mainly
through consolidations.[19] During the same period, the Senate Finance Subcommittee on Health announced it would hold hearings
to review PSRO administration and operation. Its purpose was to
find PSROs that were not cost-effective and replace them with others that were.[20]

In late 1979, PSROs were doing only about 27 percent of actual
reviews; they had delegated the right back to 73 percent of the 4,300
hospitals in the review program. Hospitals preferred this arrangement to being reviewed by outsiders. PSROs preferred it because
delegated review costs were reimbursed out of Medicare Trust Funds
while non-delegated ones came out of their own. As a result of attempts to cut Medicare costs, this agreeable arrangement was being
threatened. The per case pay for delegated hospitals was reduced
from a suggested but not mandated $13.00 per case to a mandated
$8.70.[21] Hospitals began to give up their delegated status, turning
the responsibility back to the PSROs, thus creating enormous
problems of both volume and cost. As one physician observed in a
letter to *American Medical News*, a mechanism existed for getting rid
of PSROs: "Bankrupt them. If enough hospitals elected a complete
nondelegated review, the total cost of that review would be borne
by PSROs. They can't afford it."[22]

This letter attests to the unpopularity of utilization review among
physicians. However, all were not hostile to PSRO, which was
coming to represent an entirely new element in the health care system. Those who worked within that new element were intent on
their own survival. Industry's goal of extending PSRO to the private sector had enjoyed some success. By 1979, 25 percent of existing PSROs had contracts with private insurers to review private
patients.[23] Insurance companies were responding to corporate demands for stringent review policies. Consequently, an entirely new,
centralized industry was growing up around peer review. Both PSRO
and Foundations for Medical Care formed umbrella organizations
to set up national peer and utilization review networks to work un-

der private contracts with businesses.[24] A number of companies began negotiating such agreements, including Continental, United,
American, and Frontier Airlines and other corporations.[25]

Reports in the provider press indicate that the physician community was effectively split on this issue. For example, the medical
director of the Torrance, California, PSRO stated publicly that the
process of utilization review had been hampered by the anxiety and
hostility of both physicians and hospitals to any perceived form of
government intervention.[26]

Physicians such as these, who actually worked in PSROs, appear
to have had some power within their professional organizations; the
AMA even expressed concern over the loss of PSRO funding.[27]

In some places, peer review began to function as originally intended. One Washington, D.C., PSRO warned the physicians in its
area that it might not pay either physicians or hospitals for fifty-one
surgical procedures done on in-patients if their review concluded
they could be done on an out-patient basis.[28]

In 1979 an analysis of 1977 figures by HEW revealed that some
PSROs had been more effective than others. (The 1977 HEW report that found no cost-efficiency was for the period ending in January of that year.) HEW estimated that the ninety-six PSROs operating in 1977 spent $45 million and saved $50 million, a net gain
of $5 million. Medicare beneficiaries in PSRO areas used 1.5 per-
cent fewer days of hospital care than in those without them.[29] The
PSROs were saving some money, although the figures suggest they
were bailing out a leaking boat with a sieve. However, for industry,
with its systems approach, cutting costs was only part of the goal.

Industry used peer and utilization review in far more sophisticated and strategic ways than government ever could have done, for
many complex reasons.

First, the government was itself part of the structural system that
supported physician dominance. It was the source of legal monopolies and massive funds; it was subject to the lobbying apparatus of
the AMA, which was very strong; and in dealing with professionals, as in dealing with industry, government put most of its regulatory mechanisms in the hands of the regulated.

Second, there existed no mandates through which government
could control other causes of rising health care costs simultaneously

with peer review. Government was not flexible enough to attempt to restructure the entire system, nor was it inclined to do so.

Third, existing legislation mandated review only for publicly funded health services and left the private sector untouched. Government was unwilling to take the political risk of attempting to ration the services of employed, middle-class people. This was unacceptable to industry, which understood that, given the size and structure of the health care system, the losses providers suffered in public receipts would be passed on to the private sector, leaving health care cost inflation untouched. Industry is intimately familiar with both this practice and its outcome. The need for a holistic approach was obvious.

Fourth, even for publicly funded patients government could not cut the health delivery services it had so recently declared were the right of all citizens. Such a move would have generated enormous political heat at that time. Even industry was unwilling to take such a position overtly; instead it used peer and utilization review to justify cuts in services only on the grounds that they were medically unnecessary. It would attack the rights issue in another time and place.

Although government had been unable to make practical use of its legislative enactments, they performed invaluable functions for industry's strategy to undermine physician control of the health care system. The underlying assumption of the legislation, that overutilization was the major cause of massive health care cost inflation, called into question the legitimating bases of physician autonomy: its service ethic and knowledge claims. The implications were damning and inescapable. Overutilization could have no other basis than professional greed, ignorance, or a weak tendency to indulge the self-destructive proclivities of patients. Although it served virtually no other real function at that time, the "anti-fraud and abuse amendments" passed by Congress in 1977 helped establish the idea that physicians must be watched and controlled just like any other recipient of government funds.

In 1983 this concept was so well established that the Department of Health and Human Services (HHS) could hire a former FBI agent, Richard P. Kusserow, to launch a new "anti-fraud drive." Kusserow functions as the " 'policeman' of the Mediplans." To ensure that

this drive is more effective than its predecessors, Kusserow has at
his command a very valuable new weapon, "a law that allows it [the
HHS] to levy a civil penalty of $2,000 for each false claim filed plus
twice the amount falsely claimed, without taking the provider to
court."[30]

Kusserow will use several tactics for pinpointing wrongdoers, including tips from third-party payers processing Medicare claims,
Medicaid fraud control units, and private citizens. His most powerful tool, however, will be sophisticated computer programs created to detect violations. Kusserow sees his work as extending far
beyond HHS; he wants to share both techniques and computer data
bases with private insurers "to prevent fraud from being recycled
from one sector to another." In July 1982 his office held a conference for third-party payers titled "Harnessing Technology to Fight
Health Provider Fraud and Abuse." A national center for information sharing on computer applications was created as one result of
this meeting. The emergence of this use of the computer will be
discussed in detail below.

Now that physician supervision has been established as a principle, industry can use it in much more far-reaching ways than could
government. That is why it was willing to help pay for peer review,
which has always been very expensive. Policing the system costs nearly
as much as overutilization. The issue of comparative costs was addressed early by the Series, but the assumption was made that once
peer review had served its function of helping to rationalize the health
care structure, internal mechanisms would prevent overutilization
rather than cause it. At that point, the formal review system would
become unnecessary and would, presumably, wither away.

This view has proven prophetic. In 1982 Congress repealed the
law that created peer review as a result of the Reagan administration's recommendation that federal funding be phased out. Peer review itself is in no danger of disappearing, however; it will be replaced by the new peer review organizations (PROs), which will
continue to win private contracts wherever their efforts prove to be
cost-effective. They will be highly centralized, usually one for each
state rather than the old PSRO network of 203 designated areas
throughout the country. They will not be either controlled or funded
by the federal government, however. In a stroke of near genius, the
cost of review is being handed back to physicians themselves. The

medical societies will have first shot at becoming the designated PROs within their own states, but they will have to establish a funding base in order to do so.[31] Motivated by a wish to regain control of peer review, physicians have been neatly manipulated into paying for the process that has contributed so importantly to their own loss of autonomy.

OVERUTILIZATION AND PEER REVIEW

By "overutilization," industry has described two kinds of practices. First, it is the overuse of hospital facilities, both in-patient and out-patient, for diagnostic, treatment, and surgical procedures that could be performed in less costly settings, such as the doctor's office. This is the kind of overutilization the peer review provisions of Medicare and Medicaid were originally intended to prevent.

Second, it includes delivery of any diagnostic, treatment, or surgical procedures in any kind of facility for either publicly or privately insured patients that could be defined as "unnecessary." This is a far more comprehensive view of overutilization than the first. The first peer review units did not demonstrate that unnecessary care was delivered.[32] Analysts adduced indirect evidence for its existence, such as wide variations in patterns of hospital utilization rates and lengths of stay across the country; significantly lower hospital admission rates for members of prepaid group practice plans than for members of traditional plans, without negative effects on health status; and reductions in surgical rates when second-opinion surgery programs were implemented.

Many other explanations could have accounted for these variations, of course. For example, differential hospital utilization rates cross-country could be explained on the basis of cultural, occupational, and demographic factors; it is possible that the members of prepaid group practice plans represent different populations than members of traditional plans, as discussed in chapter 4; and it was not yet known what would be the health outcome of reductions in surgery rates.

Industry is well aware that it has extended the original meaning and intent of peer and utilization review. The Series states that as data are collected, new ways to use them in the review procedure are being found: "In some instances multiple and repeated injec-

tions or treatments stand out as beyond the broad band of acceptable medical practice. In others, hospital lengths of stay."[33]

What is new is that utilization review has been expanded to include such treatment procedures as injections. The goal is now to
use peer review not only to combat overutilization but to standardize practice. This is both necessary and inevitable in order to define
services as "unnecessary." Industry's strategy is to use peer pressure,
supported by administrative processes and a computerized data base,
to create standardized treatment procedures, to ensure the widespread use of those procedures through reimbursement incentives,
and then to adduce the fact that they are in widespread use as evidence that they constitute the best available medical practice.

DATA, STATISTICS, AND STANDARDS

PSRO made necessary the creation of a data base capable of supporting its own underlying assumptions. It would include centralized information about patients, hospitals, physicians, utilization and
treatment trends and effectiveness, and other data. Industry believed that this data had the potential to justify its claims that physician control had resulted in the creation of a health care system
that was inefficient, wasteful, and, it was even argued, harmful to
the health of patients.

This use of data touches upon an important principle in medical
practice: patient-doctor confidentiality. It is a principle upon which
major techniques for maintaining professional authority are based.
Violating it seriously undermines both mystification of the knowledge base and claims by professionals that their decisions are ra-
tionally and ethically based. It could also have immediate and dangerous practical consequences for physicians. First, if all medical
diagnostic and treatment information were statistically correlated and
publicly reported, as industry desires, any deviation from these
published norms by any physician might be seen as either incompetence or malpractice. This could lead to malpractice suits. Second, the criteria and standards could come to be used as "definitive
measures" of malpractice once they were published, even though they
were supposedly intended only for screening purposes.[34]

This is the way industry wishes to use health care data. Conversely, it is just this use of data that physicians fear most; that is
why they want to control it.

The concept of standards is complex; it is often used in a double sense. It refers to both criteria and process. It provides the criteria for the acceptance of some specific medical procedures as superior to others strictly on the basis of their outcomes, evaluated in terms of health, cost-efficiency, or both. At the same time, it refers to the process of defining those medical procedures, entailing the standardization of medical practice, on the basis of data. The data base, the standards, and the enforcement of standards all emerged together as features of the process of cost control

The Series reflects a circularity of reasoning about medical standards. First, it claims that due to professional opposition and a reimbursement system that did not require it, health care diagnostic and treatment data do not exist. That is why it must be collected and organized now, in order to evaluate outcomes and determine what the highest standards could be.

Second, the Series denies the common charge that the standardization of medical diagnosis and treatment results in mechanical, dehumanizing services and evokes images of "Big Brother," by claiming that this cannot be so because the standards already exist: "800 medical societies, specialty boards, and government authorities *already* promulgate them."[35] However, this is a little-known fact. Third, although these nonexistent data-based standards *do* exist, they are so contradictory as to be useless; they are not available to physicians and their organizations in any consistent, standardized form.[36]

These are all seen as reasons why medical standards are very ambiguous. However, the Series maintains, unambiguous standards could exist if the attempt were made to collect and disseminate data. In 1977 it cited Henry Damm of Damm and Associates, who maintained that "health services can be measured in terms as precise as the industrial products being scrutinized every day through quality control systems."[37]

Damm's goal was to establish such a system, a national data base that would simultaneously determine and enforce standards for all diagnostic and therapeutic procedures. It would gather data from all hospitals on all treatments, diagnoses, and outcomes, on the basis of which it would establish treatment standards. Once the statistically valid data base is established, any diagnostic or treatment procedures would be screened against its standards, all the while creating more data and setting new standards. This is exactly the kind of data base that was put to use by Kusserow at HHS in 1983.

Damm worked with a number of employers, including TRW, AT&T, Sun Company, Uniroyal, Dayco, and Sears, to establish this system. He believed that it would eliminate the need for second opinions, since all procedures would be statistically valid, and that it would also eliminate or greatly reduce malpractice suits, since all procedures, regardless of outcomes, would have followed statistically valid standards. Damm called this procedure establishing "medical-legal" as well as "medical-scientific" validity in order to establish "loss-control" by "purchasers."[38]

Damm opposed the organized PSROs because they did not utilize his unambiguous statistical approach or focus on medical-legal validity. He considered them "a throwback to the outdated community standard of practice," which is based on consensus of opinion of experts, not on statistics.[39]

Of course, even conventional peer and utilization review requires data against which to evaluate utilization patterns. Systems such as Damm's can provide data, but they must be implemented if industry's goals are to be met. Industry uses reimbursement policies to enforce the implementation of these new standards through the apparatus of PSRO. Private insurance companies that contract with PSROs may refuse to reimburse providers for procedures that are not approved by them. Thus reimbursement is the ultimate control. After a decade of peer and utilization review, the kind of data base that industry wants does exist, to some extent. However, it is in the hands of insurance carriers.

Industry complains that insurance carriers either cannot or will not provide them with the data required for rational planning. The insurance industry regards such data as a costly "product," which it does not wish to give away.[40] Perhaps just as important, an assumption of moral responsibility has accompanied control of the data. This is a systemic paradox. Just as providers claimed superior technical knowledge and the service ethic to justify monopolization of the data base, insurance companies now claim that they are more competent to evaluate the data than industry or even, possibly, providers. Thus, it was to protect the confidentiality of medical records that Steven Sieverts, of Blue Cross and Blue Shield of Greater New York, argued against corporate access to such data in 1979.[41]

But powerful corporations were demanding that carriers provide them with the requisite data for both claims management and evaluation of experimental cost containment programs.[42] These corporations wanted two kinds of data: (1) base-line utilization information for both providers and patients, which could inform a claims review system but for the early stage would be designed to tell the corporations where their problems were; and (2) more specialized information to allow industry to evaluate the results of some of the experimental cost containment programs they had caused to be implemented, such as second surgical opinions.[43] Industry believes it pays for this research, in the form of premiums and fees, and it wants to see what it has bought.

In June 1978 the Center for Industry and Health Care held a conference organized around the specific issue of how management could get the data it needed "to monitor the use of employee health benefits."[44] The conference was convened to explore the possibilities of self-insurance for corporations.

SELF-ADMINISTERED AND SELF-INSURED BENEFIT PROGRAMS

Under conventional insurance arrangements, which were nearly universal twenty years ago, insurance carriers provide all administrative services, such as enrolling members, filling out forms, and providing actuarial and legal services. They also collect premiums, which contain a number of components, including: the amount that is earmarked for claims payments, which is actuarially determined, and covers the costs to the insurance company of doing business (including state premium taxes, which usually run about 2 percent of the premium); administrative charges; risk charges, which protect the carrier from being caught with insufficient funds to pay incurred claims in case of contract terminations; and reserve funds to protect against abnormally high volumes of claims during the benefit year.

These reserves are required by state law, although the amounts vary by state and by type of plan. For conventional plans, it comes to about 20 percent of paid claims per year, sometimes a little more.

Clearly, a sizeable portion of premiums is not paid out in benefit claims. During the last fifteen years or so, insurers considered offering alternative plans that were intended to remedy this situation. A number of developments contributed to the emergence of these plans, the first of which was the initiation of experience-rated group plans by commercial carriers in the 1940s. At first, experience rating functioned simply to reduce insurance costs by excluding high-risk populations from coverage. However experience rating is logically inconsistent with the underlying rationale of insurance, that is, minimizing loss by sharing risk; instead, it minimizes loss by minimizing risk. This leaves those who need it most without coverage while transforming the insured elite into a homogeneous pool.

This fact has not been lost on industry. The Series points out that the volume of claims from large stable groups of employed people enrolled in company health plans fluctuates very little and can be predicted with little more than the application of a standard inflation factor to last year's premium. In such cases there is really very little risk for insurance carriers to assume. Just the size of the group contracts could eliminate shared risk as the major rationale for insurance.[45]

As industry began to question the reality of risk assumption and, consequently, the need for cash reserves, it began to demand and get alternative benefit designs from insurers. The three most commonly used of these were minimum premium plans (MPPs); self-funded, administrative-services-only contracts (ASOs); and, most radically, no insurance at all. Some companies have completely self-funded and self-administered plans.

The MPP first gained widespread attention at the 1964 meeting of the American Management Association, where the plan developed by Metropolitan Life Insurance Company and Caterpillar Tractor was introduced; "Cat-Met," as it was called, was the prototype minimum premium plan.

The MPP was designed primarily to reduce state premium taxes by dividing claims liability between the carrier and the policyholder, with the latter being responsible for almost the entire amount. After the emergence of Cat-Met, carriers other than Metropolitan began to develop their own versions of MPPs.[46]

In 1970 the Equitable Life Assurance Society altered the MPP concept; it wrote a contract with the 3-M Company in Saint Paul, Minnesota, that specified that the company would bear all the risk and Equitable would provide administrative services only. Under such ASO contracts the policyholder is entirely self-funded; therefore, these contracts are not really insurance policies since there is no assumption of risk by a third party. Administrative responsibilities such as claims review, data collection, plan design, and so on are done by outside contractors, usually insurance carriers or contract adminis-trators.[47]

Self-funded and self-administered benefit plans, such as those of Goodyear and Deere and Company, are the most radical alterna-tives to conventional health insurance. The employer or multi-employer trust assumes all risk and all administrative functions.

The provider press reports that these alternative systems have in-creased in importance; the earliest motive for their development ap-pears to have been the desire for a reduction of premium costs by elimination of some taxes, of mandated benefits, and of administra-tive inefficiencies.[48]

Industry soon realized that these costs were not the core of the problem; administrative savings reached a plateau very rapidly, while health care costs continued to rise. With this realization some cor-porations began to look beyond the potential for administrative savings in alternative funding and toward their potential for direct intervention in the health care system. This approach goes much further than attempting to close the gap between premiums re-ceived and claims paid out. It attempts to reduce "both the volume and the unit costs of certain medical services." This is a clearly stated plan by corporations to use insurance initiatives to control diagnos-tic and treatment decisions carried out by physicians. The public policy implications of these moves are explicitly stated by the Se-ries: "The possibility that industry, acting independently or in col-laboration with private insurance carriers, might implement pro-grams designed to influence the volume of health care services employees demand and use has obvious ramifications for corporate policy and for public policy as well."[49] It is clear that industry per-ceives claims control to be a potential source of systemic change, affecting directly the health care services that employees demand and use.

It can also be used to control the services providers decide to de-liver. The most radical example of how an alternative insurance car-rier can exercise such control is provided by an organization called the United States Administrators (USA) in California. USA is an administrative-service-only ASO carrier. Its president, Samuel X. Kaplan, assumes a very tough stance in relation to provider control,

stating: "Either there will be a slugfest with providers or else employers will go on writing blank checks. . . . Insurance companies
don't have the guts to take the bull by the horns and do real claims
control."[50]

The computer is a crucial part of Kaplan's system. It does all the
conventional kinds of claims analysis, such as eligibility and fee checks,
but it also does much more. Kaplan commissioned a group he calls
a Council of Health Professionals made up of twenty-three physicians to establish model treatment programs (MTPs) for over four
thousand medical diagnoses.[51] Every medical encounter, either ambulatory or in-patient care, that is covered by the USA plan is accounted for in this scheme. Every claim is fed into the computer
and analyzed.

The computer utilizes established criteria to determine whether
the treatment was reasonable, given the diagnosis, age, and sex of
the patient; whether the place of service was appropriate; whether
the number of follow-up days and days in the hospital were appropriate; and so on. The computer stores huge amounts of data that
relate diagnoses to suitable treatments and indicates the frequency
of acceptable treatments.[52] It also marks any claims that surpass the
criteria it has established.

Every charge is processed through this model treatment screen,
checked against computerized fee profiles, and disallowed if the
computer says it is excessive. When patients are hospitalized, even
miscellaneous charges are screened. According to Kaplan, these
charges, which are usually ignored, make up around 50 percent of
the hospital bill. Kaplan's system uses both prospective and retrospective review. As soon as a patient is admitted to a hospital, admissions calls USA to confirm the patient's coverage and benefits
level. At that point USA asks for the admitting diagnosis and tells
the hospital what length of stay is authorized. That night the USA
computer writes a letter stating the length of stay it will allow. The
letter is sent to the attending physicians and copies are sent to both
the hospital and the patient. The letter warns that if the doctor leaves
the patient in the hospital one day longer than the time allowed
without justifying it, neither USA nor the patient will pay for it.

We'll use any kind of threat we can think of—letters to medical or dental
societies, letters and calls to the local newspaper or the local TV and radio
stations if we have to . . . whatever it takes.[53]

Kaplan maintains that simple self-insurance alone saves many large corporations from 10 to 15 percent, but those that are utilizing these review procedures are saving from 25 to 30 percent. These include H. F. Ahmanson, DelMonte, Hunt-Wesson, and Johns-Manville. He urges that every insurance company and administrator become "operational PSROs" in order to combat skyrocketing costs that corporations pay for health care.[54]

Kaplan's strategy goes far beyond peer pressure and review and borders on outright intimidation. His suggestion that insurance companies and administrators become *"PSROs"* transforms the meaning of the word "peer," substituting administrative for colleague review. The only area in which he solicited physician input was in the standardization of the four thousand diagnoses and treatment procedures; once that process was complete, the fact that it was carried out by professionals legitimates computer surveillance of medical treatment at the most minute level. Kaplan was one of the first to carry the rationalization of professional work to its ultimate conclusion. His tactics, which sounded radical even to industry in the late 1970s, are now standard procedure at HHS.[55]

STANDARDIZED CARE, STANDARDIZED COSTS

In the late 1970's there began to appear some standardized systems that made utilization and peer review seem antiquated. They were designed by commercial management consultants and utilized many of the same statistical techniques as those advocated by Damm and Kaplan.

Statistical techniques were used in delivery settings to standardize and enforce the costs of specific procedures through new reimbursement rate-setting models. Management engineers and costs accountants had developed techniques to identify all costs for a particular patient service, called a patient care unit (PCU). These costs include labor, materials, equipment, facilities, and allocated overhead.[56]

In 1976, Yale University designed the diagnosis related group (DRG), which categorizes patients into 383 groups based on their diagnosis, age, and sex. DRG no. 6286, for instance, includes patients with appendicitis who are under ten years old.

By 1979 the Illinois Hospital Association was collecting data and testing a system designed by a Chicago-based management firm that

used these PCUs and DRGs to establish a new kind of hospital
reimbursement system. Each hospital would develop its own PCU
costs to provide for variations in facilities and local wage rates. These
derived costs would then be compared with the hospital's actual costs
to determine whether productivity targets were being met.

In this system, reimbursements are based on the patients' diagnoses and the PCUs assigned them rather than on services actually
delivered. Thus, it institutionalizes the prospective review system so
opposed by physicians. Providers are not rewarded for delivering
unnecessary services, which are defined as those not included in the
calculations for PCUs and DRGs.

Those who were involved with the early stages of testing and establishing this process were aware of the effects they would have on
professional practice and attitudes. Martin Drebin, Vice President
of Finance at Evanston Hospital, told *Modern Healthcare* that PCUs
were "the basis for the most intelligent reimbursement system ever
invented" but added that they would have to be "promoted carefully to allay any fears that treatment standards are being fixed by
the government or hospital management."[57]

These programs were expected to be self-enforcing. Timothy
Garton, Illinois Hospitals' Association Project Director for the study,
says, "I think that they [physicians] will impose some controls on
themselves and that a natural process of 'convergence to the mean'
will occur."[58]

Between 1980 and 1983 the DRG system was put into effect on
a test basis over all the state of New Jersey. Although it did not cut
costs significantly, President Reagan signed into law as part of the
Social Security Amendments of 1983 a bill that mandates implementation of the DRG prospective review system in hospital billing
for all Medicare patients all over the country by 1986. This follows
the same course as that taken earlier to stimulate development of
PSROs.

This is an extremely important move for several reasons. First, of
course, is the fact that the federal government mandates the system
for all Medicare hospital patients. This virtually ensures that DRGs
will be applied to privately funded cases as well, just as peer and
utilization review procedures were developed for publicly funded
patients and extended to cover those who are privately funded as
well. Business coalitions are working very actively to speed this pro-

cess. For example, in Arizona the four largest employers—Honey-well, Inc.; Sperry Corp.; Motorola, Inc.; and Garrett Corpora-tion—formed the Arizona Coalition for Cost-Effective Quality Health Care, which now has one thousand member employers. The coali-tion backed a bill that would require hospitals to use a uniform bill-ing system based on DRGs by February 1, 1984. Governor Bruce Babbitt recently signed the bill into law over the active opposition of the Arizona Hospital Association.[59]

Second, although DRGs are supported by the federal govern-ment, they do not represent a regulatory form. Like HMOs, they incorporate controls on the basis of managerial decisions and forms that are based on statistical analysis. They are, in effect, a federally mandated and funded, unregulated billing system driven by market forces.

Young and Saltzman believe that presently there is no "top man-agement" in hospitals, but rather a system that is "bifurcated into medical and financial lines of authority," each of which is character-ized by incentives to use resources in self-interested ways guaran-teed to defeat cost-cutting initiatives.[60] Thus they, like many oth-ers, explain the fact that rate-setting systems have failed to control health care costs in the past because of this dual authority arrange-ment. They propose a new kind of "matrix management system" in which rate setting would function as a form of top management that would exercise "strategic and operational control over both admin-istrators and physicians." Thus if rate setting is effective at all, it will be because it functions as a formularized system to control ad-ministrative and management decisions.

Now that the concept of peer review is well established, it legit-imates a variety of systems for the rationalization of health care. Af-fected are both actual treatments and the settings in which they are delivered, which may now be either traditional or new alternative settings. Among these alternative settings are ambulatory care units and surgicenters, which are out-patient facilities for the perfor-mance of minor surgeries that in the past have been performed in hospitals.

PEER REVIEW, THIRD-PARTY PAYMENTS, AND
ALTERNATIVE FACILITIES

The "appropriate settings" provisions of peer review were intended to prevent hospitalization for treatment and diagnostic procedures that could be done elsewhere at a lower cost. Unnecessary
hospitalization had become routine for a long list of diagnostic and
treatment procedures.

Although the emergence of the hospital system must be attributed to many complex factors, industry believes hospitals became the major settings for health care delivery as a result of badly
conceived reimbursement policies. Because of these policies, a health
care system developed without physical alternatives to hospitals.
Hospital beds proliferated, begging to be filled, while there existed
very few clinics where even minor surgeries could be performed. In
recent years even primary care physicians delivering out-patient services have been disappearing, forcing increasing numbers of patients into expensive hospital emergency rooms for routine care. As
remedies for this situation, industry supports the development of
alternative treatment settings and the delivery of primary care by
paraprofessionals and nurses.

Industry succeeded in persuading insurance carriers to pay for
procedures done in ambulatory care units and surgicenters, which
promptly began to increase in numbers. Government was slower than
industry to embrace the concept. However, in the mid–1970's
Congress required HEW to conduct an impact study on free-standing
surgical centers. HEW was to compare the cost and quality of care
performed in the centers with those of the same services delivered
in hospitals. It was also required to estimate the financial impact of
the centers on the hospitals in the same areas; this provision reflects
both government sensitivity to provider lobbies and awareness of
the fact that hospitals are major employers. Hospital failures might
have widespread political as well as economic impact.

HEW found the quality of care in the centers to be as good as
care delivered to in-patients in hospitals. Costs were also lower: lowest
in free-standing units; intermediate in hospital-affiliated units; and
highest in hospitals. And the study found that no damage occurred
to existing hospitals in the area (Phoenix, Arizona) either from ambulatory care units or surgicenters.

In 1973, Robert Gordon set up a "convenience clinic" in War-wick, Rhode Island, the first in the country. By 1983 there were 650 of them in operation and they had established a professional association, the National Association of Freestanding Emergency Centers.[61] These alternative facilities serve several important func-tions in the process of restructuring the health care system. They are themselves elements of a new system existing outside the large and powerful control structures of traditional medical practice. Physicians have historically opposed many practices that are com-mon in ambulatory units, such as critical peer review and use of paraprofessional personnel. These alternative units put competitive pressure on the traditional system, which has resulted in some modifications of the structure and practice of medicine in hospitals, such as the creation of out-patient, non-emergency care facilities and the practice of contracting with physician groups to deliver care within the hospital in a more cost-effective way.

They also usually provide specific services more cheaply than do hospitals for a number of reasons: they do not include amortized expense components that would add the cost of expensive capital equipment used elsewhere in the hospital; they utilize paraprofes-sional personnel; they exercise stringent review procedures; and they treat patients who are less seriously ill than those treated in hospi-tals. For example, hospitals are thought to do renal dialysis proce-dures on older, sicker patients than do the ambulatory units.

Finally, they provide a setting in which tests that were previously done in hospitals may be provided more cheaply and without the patient being hospitalized. Industry put great pressure on hospitals to accept these tests in lieu of their own battery of admission tests, charging that they often duplicate procedures that have already been done, could be done more economically elsewhere, or were unnec-essary in the first place. Providers, they say, use tests automatically in an attempt to ward off any possible future malpractice suits.

The pressure to accept non-hospital tests has been the reimburse-ment carrot provided by insurers. It paid off. In February 1979 the Chicago-based Blue Cross and Blue Shield Association announced that reimbursement for routine admission tests on non-surgical pa-tients would no longer be made. These patients accounted for 55 percent of hospital admissions. In May 1979, *Modern Healthcare* re-ported that the Michigan Blues would be the first to implement the plan statewide, effective July 1, 1979. Michigan Blue Cross and Blue Shield went even further than the recommendation of the national organization, requiring that "medical documentation" be required for admissions tests for surgical as well as non-surgical patients. The national association then expanded its recommendation to include surgical patients, who make up 45 percent of hospital admissions.[62] Although McNerney admitted this was a cost control measure, the move was based on the assumption that by definition routine tests are not medically necessary.

Provider reactions to this measure were mixed. The American College of Physicians backed the plan and issued the statement that "the injudicious use of diagnostic tests contributes greatly to the cost of medical care."[63] Such statements reflected the increasing defensiveness of physicians, who were unwilling to make public statements in defense of procedures that they have not specifically ordered and that are not indicated by the patient's symptoms. Overall, however, the provider press presented an image of division among physicians on this issue. Clearly many did see the tests as deterrents to malpractice suits: "McNerney's announcement sparked bitter reaction from some physicians' groups which insist that the routine tests are necessary for protection from the everpresent malpractice threat."[64]

Hospitals also adopted a defensive stance. The Joint Commission on Accreditation of Hospitals denied that its standards require routine clinical laboratory tests or X-ray examinations for hospital admission; in making this statement, the commission indicted those hospitals that engage in the practice.[65]

Like other initiatives taken by industry, the rule eliminating reimbursement for automatic tests could be used in other ways as well. Although the original intent of the reimbursement policy was to eliminate unnecessary tests, it has also been used in an attempt to prevent unnecessary hospitalization, as demonstrated by this report of a lawsuit against Blue Cross and Blue Shield of California.

At a hearing scheduled for later this month, the plan will contest the arbitrator's decision to award more than $313,000—$300,000 for punitive damages, $12,000 for emotional and mental distress and $1,116 for unpaid hospital charges—to an insured patient whose claim for diagnostic tests was refused because the Plan said the patient's hospitalization was unnecessary. The Plan claimed the tests could have been done on an out-patient basis.[66]

Thus inappropriate setting provisions enable insurers to disallow diagnostic tests without denying their medical necessity if they were performed in the wrong place, in a hospital. This provides an example of the ways original intent can be altered, so that mechanisms created for a specific purpose may be utilized innovatively, in a variety of situations.

EDUCATING HEALTH CARE USERS

Industry approaches health care information for consumers who are real or potential patients from two perspectives. The first concerns lifestyle, that is, personal habits that affect health. The second is consumer education directed toward making people aware of the costs of their health care decisions and training them to question their physicians about costs, to get second opinions to determine whether recommended procedures are medically necessary, and to try to get the "best buy" in health care, as they would when shopping for any other service.

Instead of attacking head-on the ideology that health care is a right of all citizens, industry focuses on bad personal habits of individuals. It makes the case that society cannot afford to provide health care as a right to individuals who will not take responsibility for themselves.[67] Pointing out that lifestyle is an important contributor to disability and early death, the Series singles out the workplace as a logical locus for health education and the promotion of healthful lifestyles, although it stresses that business must tread carefully in implementing such health promotion strategies, to avoid violating the civil liberties of individuals.[68]

Industry has undertaken to educate people to adopt more healthful lifestyles through political activities, advertising, and employee counseling. Political activities include creation of the National Center for Health Education in October 1975 at the recommendation of the President's Committee on Health Education. The committee was formed in 1971. It was chaired first by Joe Wilson of Xerox and then by R. Heath Larry of U.S. Steel Corporation.[69] The center itself generated so much interest in the corporate sector that it was created even before federal funding was assured.

Since that time, the federal government has actively promoted the concepts of health education and consumer self-help. It enacted the National Consumer Health Education and Health Promotion Act

of 1976 (P.L. 94–317), which provides on a national basis information about healthful practice, preventive health services, and appropriate ways in which to use health care services.[70] It also enacted
the Health Services Research, Health Statistics, and Health Care
Technology Act of 1978 (P.L. 95–623). This legislation author-
izes, in part, the activities of the National Center for Health Services Research,[71] which solicits grant applications for all types of
preventive health care research and publishes reports on consumer
self-care in health.[72]

The health insurance industry has also been promoting self-help.
Advertising initiatives have been launched by the Health Insurance
Institute, a public relations firm that represents the Health Insurance Association, an organization representing over three hundred
health insurance companies. The public relations firm developed
advertisements that focused on six "promising areas," combining
"national advertising and public relations on a scale never before attempted" in that business.[73]

The six promising areas include (1) the creation of more hospital
budget review commissions; (2) the adoption of effective certificate
of need programs in every state; (3) a greater self-responsibility for
health on the part of the individual; (4) recruiting "knowledgeable"
people to serve in the health planning process; (5) stressing alternatives to hospital care, such as HMOs, outpatient centers, and so
on; and (6) encouraging second opinions and outpatient surgical
services. All these targets for a national advertising campaign are
initiatives aimed at by industry.

Industry promotes "mental health" treatment as a way of com-
bating unhealthy lifestyles.[74] Ford and Pittsburgh Plate Glass do al-
cohol and drug abuse counseling and out-patient treatment for their
employees.[75] Continental Bank has planned an extremely comprehensive employee education program, which includes identifying and
treating employees with "personal problems"; running clinics for
smoking, hypertension screening, diabetes detection, and weight
reduction; publishing articles in the company newspaper about good
health practices; outlining nutritional programs for the firm's food
service areas and for individuals with specific medical needs; running seminars to reduce and control stress, focusing on areas such
as vocational needs, marital conflict, divorce, teenage drug abuse,
mental health, and child care; and providing facilities for aerobic

exercises to improve the cardiovascular and pulmonary systems of employees.[76]

Continental Bank has had some problems with the implementation of this program. First, job-site intervention can be expected to have only limited impact on the larger health care system. Second, it is difficult to get people to make permanent changes in their behavior patterns. Third, Continental Bank recognizes that some of its initiatives would themselves be prohibitively expensive, because, for example, "healthy eating is more expensive than 'junk food' eating," and many people will not exercise unless they get time off work to do it.[77] Fourth, such a program is apt to be resented as paternalistic: "We cannot overlook the American tradition of freedom of choice. We imagine that it would be simpler to apply such ideas as we suggest in a German or a Russian Factory than in an American Bank."[78]

Continental Bank is not deterred, however. It counts among its blessings the fact that for the most part its workers are not unionized: "This gives us greater leeway in our planning."[79] The bank has a personnel health insurance administrator who consults with employees before they go into the hospital and advises them about usual charges. The bank tells the patient in advance how much his or her insurance will pay. Before their consultations with these administrators, the employee must obtain detailed prices and treatment plans from their physicians. "Many people consider this bad form but our health education program will point out that they may be surprised after the fact by what the insurance pays."[80] Thus the employee is "motivated by an uncertain personal expenditure" to question the doctor about charges beforehand.[81] Thus the bank utilizes economic incentives to encourage the habit of questioning professional decisions, knowledge, and ethics.

Continental Bank also believes the employee-patient can learn to do his or her own quality and utilization review. The procedure appears to be complex, particularly for a person who is presumably somewhat incapacitated. The bank plans to work with the Chicago Foundation for Medical Care to implement a utilization review program in which employees will be trained to apply statistics on length of stay norms to do the review.[82]

Some corporations have utilized a more directly economic approach to changing employee utilization patterns. Mobil Oil reported in 1977 that it gives a monthly bonus to groups of employees who have lowered their utilization rates.[83] By 1981, Blue Shield of California was underwriting a test plan in Ukiah, California, that attempts to reduce health care costs by paying subscribers up to $500 not to go to the doctor: "a deductible of $500 is credited to each subscriber. Any amount left at the end of the year is saved until the subscriber leaves or retires from the system."[84]

Many corporations are looking into ways to get more (and new) provisions for co-insurance and deductibles, although this was at first considered very difficult. Great public hostility was expected if benefits were taken away once they were implemented. However, as Goldbeck pointed out in 1977, less than 25 percent of the work force is unionized and of that number only about 40 percent have coverage that is totally paid by the employer. He concluded that it is not too late to turn things around; the first step is to stop negotiating new coverage.[85] The more recent and familiar trend has been toward labor union "give backs" of many negotiated benefits, including health care insurance, although to date no public revolt has been forthcoming.

SUMMARY

Insurers have experienced pressure from many segments of the larger health care environment to intervene in the health care system and to contain costs. These pressures have acted alone and in interaction to induce controlling behavior on the part of insurance companies; they include (1) the emergence of industry as a health care consumer with enormous economic and political power that negotiates insurance contracts for millions of employees; (2) government attacks on the bond between the Blues and providers in the form of anti-trust suits, which are supported by industry; (3) market competition from non-traditional or non-regulated insurers; (4) the institutionalization of collective bargaining with its concomitant fringe benefits; (5) the trend in industry to self-insure to achieve its goals; (6) the development of PSROs, which provide both data to legitimate the insurers' cost containment initiatives and support from at least some providers for a "get tough" policy by insurers.

The traditional insurance industry has responded to these pres-

sures by implementing policies that undermine professional dominance of the health care sector. As a result the positions of both
traditional providers and insurance carriers are weakened. Historically, each had maintained its power position through supportive
ties to the other. These ties are in the process of dissolution.

3

Industrial Health Programs

The term industrial health program (IHP) refers to facilities owned and controlled by corporations for the delivery of health care services to their employees. IHPs vary in the ranges of services they provide. Some corporations do little more than screen employees known to have been exposed to hazardous substances. Others schedule employee examinations on the basis of epidemiological and demographic factors that have been shown to be statistically related to pathology and then use those test results to practice in-house preventive medicine. These in-house services include both the delivery of medical treatment and attempts to alter employee lifestyles through corporate educational programs and psychological counseling.

Since the late 1960's, industry has had increasingly good reason to function as a direct provider of health care services. By doing so it can avoid the costs of rising insurance premiums, participate more effectively in planning health care delivery services that are cost-effective, exercise increased control over health care professionals (who are often employees), and collect and control certain vital employee health care data and statistics. Passage of the Occupational Safety and Health Act of 1970 created an even stronger motivation for industry to become a provider. OSHAct requires industry to collect health care data for employees known to have been exposed to hazardous substances and to inform those employees both of the exposure and of any pathology discovered by the screening. All this data must be made available to the Occupational Safety and Health Administration. In addition, commercial manufacturers, processors, or distributors of chemical substances must inform the administration of the Environmental Protection Agency if they have any information indicating that the substances or mixtures they handle represent substantial risks of injury to either their workers' health or the environment.[1]

By functioning as a provider, industry can deliver the required screening procedures in-house; this is much cheaper than having them done on the outside by private practitioners. More importantly, it stands a greater chance of maintaining control over the potentially explosive employee health statistics these screenings could generate.

HISTORICAL DEVELOPMENT OF IHPs

Contemporary IHPs are extensions of the specialty of occupational medicine that developed along with the workers' compensation programs initiated during the first two decades of this century. At that time, technological developments, rapid industrialization, industry's push to maximize production, and a labor force consisting of impoverished migrants desperately competing for work combined to make the workplace extremely hazardous. Intense labor activity and workplace tragedies such as the Triangle Shirtwaist Company fire in 1911, all of which were thoroughly detailed by muckraking journalists, stimulated widespread public indignation.[2]

Labor used the favorable publicity from the press to launch lawsuits against employers of disabled workers, often winning sizeable settlements. More importantly, the suits stimulated further public support for labor's ultimate goal, which was to force employers to create a safer workplace. Employers lobbied for a more palatable alternative—passage of the federal Workmen's Compensation Program, which was put forward in 1907 and enacted over labor's opposition in 1912. It is true that the AMA opposed and helped defeat early health insurance legislation.[3] However, corporate America had a far more immediate and practical economic interest in these events. As Berman points out, "Monopoly corporations such as U.S. Steel responded to the movement around occupational safety and health by setting up a business-controlled 'compensation safety apparatus,' a stalling operation which, by appearing to be doing something, withheld the issue of working conditions from the public agenda until the late 1960's."[4]

This "compensation safety" apparatus emphasized compensation over safety and contained no enforcement mechanisms for cleaning up the workplace. It was made up of a complex of business-dominated organizations concerned with compensation, workplace inspection, standards setting, research, and education in occupational health. In 1920 the Bureau of Labor Statistics developed a method for counting industrial injuries. In 1926 the method was turned over to a standards-setting group controlled by private industry. In the next forty years it went through four revisions, making it useless as a comparative base for measuring the number of work-related injuries.[5] This group was the predecessor of the American National Standards Institute (ANSI), an "umbrella organization that serves to legitimize standards developed by private industry in many areas besides occupational safety and health."[6]

Federal compensation authority decisions were based on these standards, even when good evidence indicated they were wrong. For example, for decades state and federal compensation authorities denied that coal dust was a hazard, although black lung was recognized as a compensable disease in Britain in 1943.[7] It was recognized as such in the United States only after intense political activity by a coalition of miners, widows, physicians, and certain members of Congress resulted in passage of the federal Coal Mine Health and Safety Act of 1969.

Consistently lower safety and exposure levels have been recommended by industry as opposed to non-industry controlled research. The case of asbestos provides an infamous example.

By 1969, sixty-three scientific papers on the problems of asbestos exposure and health had been published in the United States, Great Britain and Canada. The fifty-two papers published independently of the asbestos industry showed asbestos to be a dangerous source of asbestosis and lung cancer; the eleven sponsored by industry presented virtually the opposite conclusions, rejecting the connection between asbestos exposure and cancer and minimizing the seriousness of asbestosis.[8]

Workers' compensation cannot serve to reduce workplace health hazards while industry controls the setting of standards. Rather, it

functions to pension off disabled workers at a fraction of their previous earnings. The National Commission of State Workman's
Compensation Laws estimates that in 1972, fours years before passage of the OSHAct provided any possible alternative to workers'
compensation, "the median percentage of wage loss replaced in
temporary total disability cases was 40–44%."[9] Despite this extreme loss of income just when it is most needed, workers' compensation laws prohibit workers from suing for damages if their
disabilities are found to be occupationally caused! Only very recently have courts begun to award workers who already receive
workers' compensation the right to sue employers directly for occupationally caused injuries or illness. Such decisions by the courts
represent both an economic threat and a loss of control by employers, for whom, as the *New York Times* has observed, "the workmen's compensation system has long been an important shield against
costly litigation."[10] Whether or not such suits continue to be allowed and what their impact will be on employers will be determined in large part by what kind of occupational health data is collected and who controls it.

DATA CONTROL AND OCCUPATIONAL HEALTH STANDARDS

Data control forms the basis both for the physicians' monopoly
over medical practice and for industry's power to set the standards
by which worker safety is evaluated. While physicians have historically controlled the medical records of private patients, employers
have controlled data connected with occupational safety and health,
thus enabling them to make workers' compensation function in their
own interest.

Insurance companies, universities, and hospitals, of course, also
have possession of data, but they do not directly control the kinds
of data to be collected, the extent to which it is accessible to outsiders, or the uses to which it will be put. This situation has been
changing during the last two decades, as regulations have required
providers to collect and relinquish certain patient data as a prereq-
uisite for funding. This data base is relatively new, however, while
industry has controlled information for many decades.

Industry has, of course, been able to minimize the regulatory im-

pact of OSHAct through ANSI standards. Given the current anti-
regulatory climate, it may continue to do so. The political possibilities are threatening, nevertheless. In order to fulfill its mandate,
OSHA must either support non-industry data collection and evaluation or take the political heat for setting standards acceptable to
industry but not to consumers and workers.

This heat has become increasingly intense as there accumulates
strong and mounting evidence suggesting that far more diseases,
injuries, and deaths in the United States are related to workplace
hazards and industrial pollution than official statistics have indicated: according to Ashford, they represent only the tip of the ice-
berg. Originally, occupational safety was concerned almost exclusively with workplace accidents and injuries. The more recent focus
on hazardous substances could drastically increase the numbers of
disabilities and deaths that are classified as occupationally caused.
This is so because of the vast and rapidly increasing numbers of
chemicals used in the workplace: "Approximately one-half million
chemicals are produced and used in this country, some 12,000 of
which are in widespread use throughout industry. In addition, an
estimated 3000 new chemicals are synthesized each year, with approximately 500 finding use in industry."[11]

It is expected by all observers that the kinds of data that industry
is required to collect and relinquish under OHSAct would demonstrate many connections between work and disease. Whether or not
this would result in greater numbers of increasingly stringent safety
and health regulations depends upon developing political events. In
response to "complaints" from industry in the form of lawsuits and
political pressure, OSHA and the Labor Department have proposed revisions in two important areas of OSHA regulation. One
revision would drop between 50 percent and 70 percent of the hazardous susbstances for which companies must retain records; this
would reduce the number of workers covered from more than 27
million to 16 million. The second revision would limit access by
workers or their representatives to the health records that are kept.[12]

It is this access to records by workers that has enabled them to
win the right to sue their employers, even though the provisions of
workers' compensation prohibit such suits. For example, in allowing a disabled worker to sue his employer, "the Ohio Supreme Court
ruled that workmen's compensation only protected employers from

being sued for negligent injuries, and that [the] chemical intoxication injuries could be considered intentional."[13]

Thus the court refused to accept the spirit of workers' compensation, the protection of employers from the consequences of their own negligence, by extending that protection to employers who have intentionally harmed their workers. Of course, workers must themselves prove that their employers were negligent in order to get the 40–44 percent of their income that they receive when they are totally disabled. Such proof is often difficult to obtain. However, the mandated collection of OSHA data makes the intentional nature of chemical exposures difficult to conceal. Thus industry uses every strategy it can think of to avoid either collecting or relinquishing it, including the argument that it cannot tell workers what they have been exposed to because to do so would reveal trade secrets, thus causing economic damage to the company.

Without cooperation from both the regulatory agencies and industry, popular support for OSHA counts for very little. OSHAct was enacted in a climate of great popular support. The fact that the Department of Labor adopted so few new health standards at that time (a total of four: for asbestos; for nineteen carcinogens; for coke oven emissions; and for vinyl chloride) can be explained in large part by the "lack of a firm data base with regard to exposure to toxic materials."[14] This lack of a data base was largely the result of industry's refusal to collect or release information about worker exposure and pathology. Dr. Harriet Hardy, who established the Massachusetts General Beryllium Case Registry in order to study, treat, and prevent beryllium disease testifies to this fact: "With rare exceptions industry and insurance companies withhold data on occupational disease—its character and incidence. This fact has great influence on the acquiring of knowledge of industrial illness in other as well as beryllium-using industry in the United States."[15]

Because the profits of insurance companies were at stake, the case of asbestos provides a partial exception to this rule. In 1918, United States and Canadian insurance companies stopped selling personal life insurance policies to asbestos workers, explicitly recognizing that asbestos is a health hazard, in order to protect their own profits. Undaunted by this fact, the asbestos industry continued to deny that asbestos was a health hazard for the next fifty-five years.

Asbestos has been a very profitable industry. Johns-Manville, the leading corporation in the asbestos industry, "increased its annual sales from $40 million to over $1 billion" between 1925 and 1974. During this period thousands of new uses were developed for asbestos, and the industry became a major employer. Berman reported in 1978 that ninety thousand people were working with the substance directly and another five million worked with asbestos-containing products. Since these workers brought asbestos home on their clothes, their families were exposed to it as well. At this point, most Americans have asbestos fibers in their lungs.[16]

The industry responded to mounting evidence of the hazards of asbestos by funding research of its own primarily designed to discredit reports of the danger.[17] It was the academic researchers, Dr. Irving J. Selikoff and his associates of the Mount Sinai School of Medicine, who in the 1960's traced the effects of asbestos exposure in workers without having to use corporate records.

Organized labor and consumer groups, armed with Selikoff's research findings, demanded a clean-up of both the workplace and the overall environment in the late 1960's. It was largely as a result of these activities and of testimony before the Senate by Selikoff and other professionals, who were also public dissenters, that OSHAact passed; later, an asbestos standard was set in compliance with the recommendations of private researchers over the continuing opposition of industry. It is worth pointing out, as Berman does, that the professional dissenters involved in this movement were "physicians in research or private practice who were immune or indifferent to direct economic pressure from companies."[18]

The Series refers to the liability associated with occupational health hazards as "management's sword of Damocles."[19] The experience of the asbestos industry provides a classic example that this is so. By the end of 1978 there were more than one thousand lawsuits against it, the largest being a $1 billion class-action suit that was filed for five thousand shipyard workers against fifteen asbestos manufacturers. The suit was launched just at a time when George Miller (D-Calif.), Acting Chairman of the House Subcommittee on Compensation, Health and Safety, charged that the asbestos industry had been engaged in a "cover-up" of the health dangers related to asbestos since at least 1934. Miller based his charges on certain documents obtained by his subcommittee. These included letters

written as early as 1934 urging researchers to delete from their asbestos studies data that would compromise the industry.[20]

Despite all this, almost a decade after Selikoff's findings were made
public, both officials and occupational physicians at Johns-Manville
were still denying the connection between asbestos and lung cancer. Paul Kotin, M.D., the company's Senior Vice President for
Health, Safety and Environment, said as late as 1978, "The clinical
evidence shows that lung cancer in asbestos workers is virtually limited to those who smoke cigarets. . . . lung cancer as an asbestos-
related disease would not be a problem were it not for cigaret
smoking."[21]

While she was a congressional representative for New Jersey,
Millicent H. Fenwick filed legislation to exempt from liability those
industries whose workers have suffered death and disability as a result of on-the-job exposure to asbestos. Fenwick's legislation would
have substituted federal compensation for corporate liability.[22] When
this attempt failed, the Johns-Manville Corporation sued the United
States, asserting that the government, as an employer, did not protect shipyard workers during World War II and that, as a result, the
asbestos industry is now being forced to pay the cost as a result of
class-action suits. According to Johns-Manville representatives, the
government had information it did not give the asbestos industry,
thus causing it to unwittingly expose its own workers.[23]

The Series acknowledges that industry has deceived workers both
unwittingly and deliberately. Still, it concludes that it is the lack of
scientific standards that is the basic source of confusion. The real
issue at this point, according to the Series, is that scientific evidence
is not "convincing" enough to necessitate passing it on to workers
or to indicate that modifications in the workplace are required.[24]
Yet it is industry itself that has historically controlled that evidence.
Industry's opposition to the release of data is based on its recognition of the fact that data functions to substantiate legislative claims
for the legal liability. He who controls data controls both science
and the law.

The Series displays great sociological sophistication in its analysis
of the ways in which data monopolization serves the interests of
physicians. In contrast, it does not analyze industry's use of data in
this way. Instead, it focuses on the costs to industry of compliance

with health and safety regulation, the legal mazes established by regulation, and the problems of communication with workers who have been exposed to hazards.

INDUSTRY AND OSHA

Industry has bitterly opposed both passage and implementation of OSHAct. OSHAct was meant primarily to establish and enforce the safety standards that govern the work environment in businesses under its jurisdiction.[25] Thus it threatens both industry's system of compensation and its control over information and standards.

Industry's opposition to OSHAct is documented throughout the Series. Karl Benedict, M.D., of Norton Corporation describes in detail the strategies and tactics utilized, comparing them with the "course of events that killed the National Recovery Act of Franklin D. Roosevelt's day."[26] This opposition to OSHAct and the strategies through which it was expressed make it plain that the setting of standards is subject to vast political and economic manipulation, rather than being determined by scientific knowledge. We need to destroy the myth that standards are scientifically based, says Ashford, and look instead to their social determinants. The appendix of his book includes a copy of a memo from an assistant secretary of labor under President Richard Nixon who, while directing OSHA efforts, attempted to trade "another year" of soft OSHAct implementation for campaign contributions.[27]

Of course, even after passage of OSHAct, regulatory impact has been minimal because the new agency adopted the industry-approved ANSI standards on an interim basis. However, corporate strategists must plan for the future. The problem industry now faces is how to establish new, socially legitimate techniques through which it can maintain its historical dominance in standard setting in the event that political forces undermine their support structures. Meanwhile, the Series has constructed a set of reasons why OSHA is not needed and would not work if it were.

First, the Series maintains that OSHAct will cost a lot of money without significantly affecting actual health outcomes. Current troubles have been decades building and could not, in their best judgement, have been foreseen. Furthermore, technological developments that have resulted in health hazards for a "relatively small segment of the population" are also the basis for the high standard of living attained by industrialized nations. The question really is, Do we need those products? It is unclear whose right it is to supply the answer. Society has to make some trade-offs.[28]

Health standards and regulations, in this argument, would be set in accordance with other goals than maintaining health. If we accept the Series' assumption—that exchanging the health and safety of any group of workers (conveniently defined as "small") is acceptable so that a "high standard of living" can be enjoyed by an unidentified group concealed somewhere within the concept "industrialized nation"—then talk about data is clearly irrelevant. If data do not function as the basis upon which we make informed judgements, then the only reason for collecting it must be to exploit it as a ritualistic legitimator for decisions unconnected with cause-effect rationality.

Second, the Series asserts, OSHAct is only bureaucratic duplication. Sufficient regulations already exist; what is really needed is better administration. It cites an article published in *Forbes*, titled "Toxic? To Whom," by Paul Oreffice, President of Dow Chemical, who says of OSHAct: "Dow Chemical, however, fought the bill to the end. There were already ample laws on the books to handle any problem that might arise. What's needed is better administration of the laws, not more laws."[29]

This argument ignores two basic facts. First, very few hazardous substances were covered by existing laws. Second, neither the research apparatus nor any funding source for it existed through which new substances were likely to be added to the list.

A third argument holds that OSHAct has been ineffective in setting and enforcing standards because of inadequate scientific research procedures and unsophisticated epidemiological methods.[30]

The Series does not address criticisms often made of OSHAct, namely, that it uses standards set by the industries to be regulated. Thus industry avoids looking at the socially structured features of scientific knowledge in the same way it examines the socially structured features of medical practice.

Fourth, the Series addresses the economic costs of health and safety standards. Several kinds of costs are enumerated, with a special stress on costs to the workers and to society itself, in the form of lost jobs, wages, production of goods, and the gross national product. Other costs include those associated with workplace clean-up, which could drive small or marginal businesses to bankruptcy and weaken the position of the United States in the international marketplace as a result of being forced to compete with countries unhampered by health regulations.

This argument evokes negative economic effects and blames regulations for situations that are the result of decisions and policies made by industry. Berman reports that by 1973 Amatex, an asbestos textile manufacturer, had moved all its production activities to Mexico, which, like most Third World countries, did not regulate asbestos. As a bonus for the corporation, Amatex could pay Mexican workers the country's minimum wage of five dollars per day.[31] This provides an example of the kinds of societal trade-offs the Series advocates around industrial health issues.

A relevant side topic concerns the sharing of health and safety technology between companies. Should a company that has developed production processes and engineering controls share information about controlling the effects of hazardous materials? The Series acknowledges the humanitarian issues involved in this question, stating that in a "perfect world" such "purely altruistic gestures" might, hopefully, occur.[32] However, it goes on to state that this possibility is mitigated against by the realities of a competitive marketplace, and it quotes an OSHA official who makes the same point.

When I try to be objective, I can see why a corporation might hesitate to publicize innovations in engineering controls and give up the profit edge it might otherwise enjoy. On the other hand, wouldn't it be a humane contribution to public health to pass these engineering controls around the industry, so that other workers would not have to suffer high-risk exposures?[33]

These statements indicate that processes and devices required by federal regulation to protect workers become transformed into objects of competitive advantage between corporations. That fact alone points to the weaknesses in Oreffice's argument that only better administration of existing laws is required to protect the health of workers.

Fifth, the Series argues, industry opposes OSHAct because it wishes to protect the confidentiality of employee medical records. This, it contends, is essential if the prestige of occupational medicine is to be elevated. In 1977 two corporations (a General Motors plant in Dayton, Ohio, and a DuPont Company plant in Belle, West Virginia) went to court to fight a National Institute of Occupational Safety and Health subpoena for medical records on the ground that they were protecting the privacy rights of their patient-employees. (Labor unions support the release of such information.)

This argument, if acted upon, serves the interests of industry in three ways: it withholds information from regulatory agencies that would document the existence of workplace hazards; it reverses the roles of government regulators and industry as protectors of workers' rights; and it helps establish the professional status of occupational physicians whose "expertise" legitimates the withholding of the information.

In principle, industry supports the OSHAct provision that workers must be informed of their exposures to hazardous substances. The Series states unequivocably that everyone should be informed of exposures to the substances for which OSHAct has set standards, but suggests that "levels" be set to differentiate between these "well-documented" hazards and others that are more "ambiguous." Of course, the undocumented, ambiguous category of hazards comprises the much larger set of data, due partly to the fact that industry has control of the relevant data and partly to the vast numbers of chemicals in the workplace. If workers were informed of every potential hazard, regardless of how remote the danger, too many fears would be raised unnecessarily, the Series argues.

Discussing the Fenwick bill to exempt the asbestos industry from liability and pass the costs on to the federal government, the Series states that the best way to encourage industry to release data related to health hazards in the workplace would be to establish some sort of "amnesty program." [34]

GENETIC TESTING AND OCCUPATIONAL HEALTH HAZARDS

Because the implications of data concerning occupational health hazards are so threatening to industry, it attempts to refocus the problem for the public so that the worker who gets sick rather than the workplace is blamed for the illness. Genetic testing of workers

functions in this way. A 1980 series in the *New York Times* reports
on genetic testing of workers by the petrochemical industry:[35]

Petrochemical companies have quietly tested thousands of American workers to determine if any of the genes they were born with are what industry
doctors call "defective," making the employees especially vulnerable to certain chemicals in the workplace. The process is called genetic screening.
Employers say the purpose of the tests is to provide a protective barrier,
keeping workers they term "hypersusceptible" away from industrial poi-
sons.[36]

The *Times* reported that the DuPont Company routinely screens
all blacks who apply for jobs to determine whether they are carriers
for sickle-cell anemia.

DuPont officials emphasize that the sickle trait tests do not represent discrimination against blacks and are only an effort to help them avoid potentially harmful exposure to certain chemicals. Yet the officials can offer no
firm evidence that the trait—not the disease, but only a single abnormal
gene—makes blacks more vulnerable.[37]

DuPont is in the vanguard of companies doing genetic testing, a
practice that is so controversial, the *Times* reported, that many medical directors from other companies—even those who believe that
genetic screening offers valuable possibilities—do not want to be
involved in it. (Two years later, fifty-nine corporations, many of them
among the nation's top five hundred, had informed the Congressional Office of Technology Assessment through anonymous ques-
tionnaires that they planned to begin genetic screening within five
years.)[38] Officials at DuPont, however, "feel they have the money
and the scientists to turn distrust into achievement."[39]

Non-industry researchers interviewed by the *Times* state that
screening for sickle-cell trait is useless, first, because there is no
workplace that conforms to minimal hygienic standards that would
pose problems for anyone with sickle trait[40] and, second, because
even if there were a connection, it would not begin to touch the
problem. According to Dr. Barton Childs, Chairman of the Committee for the Inborn Errors of Metabolism, which was formed in
1975 by the National Academy of Sciences to study genetic screening:

For every sickle-cell trait they can identify, we may have 1,000 more heterozygote carriers for diseases that we can't identify. . . . It shows abysmal ignorance to try to identify only that group in the population when there are so many others. . . . Many of us fear that such tests may be used as a gimmick not to clean up the workplace.[41]

Childs told the *Times* that although there was no scientific significance to the theories underlying sickle-cell testing, stigmatization of sickle-trait carriers now exists in the form of job discrimination, increased insurance premiums, and proposals to keep carriers out of the armed forces.[42]

The *Times* series reported that some researchers at Dow Chemical Company quit because of company "hostility" to their findings. Dr. Jack Kilian, Medical Director of Dow's Freeport, Texas, facilities, said that when his findings suggested that the company's methods were clean and safe, the company was happy to let him publicize them. When he and his co-workers discovered that workers who were exposed to benzene and epichlorophydrin experienced "a disturbing rate of chromosome breakage," however, officials at the company became "distant, hostile and defensive about the studies." The *Times* reports that Dow is now critical of the quality of the research carried out by Kilian and his associates. Kilian quit Dow to become a professor at the University of Texas School of Public Health. The *Times* reported that the key people who worked with him are gone, too. Meanwhile, Dow complained to the *Times* that "despite all its efforts, it still has no real data." The company planned to start the research project over from the beginning.[43]

Industry finds many uses for highly trained scientific experts as researchers into both occupational health hazards and the genetic characteristics of employees, both present and future. In both cases, professionals provide their customary services and information, while simultaneously performing a legitimating function for industry. This is the same kind of process in which professionals legitimate decisions made by bureaucratic administrators whose decisions may or may not be based on professional expertise. Occupational physicians fill these same functions.

OCCUPATIONAL PHYSICIANS

Historically, occupational physicians have played a vital role in helping industry maintain control of the workers' compensation system. Their professional monopoly, legitimated by training and a license to practice, in turn, legitimates denials of compensation claims. Occupational physicians have become increasingly important to industry since passage of OSHAct, both because it is cheaper to do the required annual screenings of workers who are at risk in-house than to comply with these requirements using outside facilities and because their professionally privileged relationship with patients can serve a new legitimating function for industry—that of maintaining corporate control of employee health care data.

Residency programs for occupational physicians take three years, only the first two of which are academic. This fact means that industry has the opportunity to "buy" residents in their third year.

During their third year, residents in occupational medicine commonly receive clinical training with a company while on salary, which orients them toward industry even before their careers have begun. This orientation has been reinforced during the past six years as the number of academic residency programs in occupational medicine has declined by nearly 50 percent while the number of in-plant programs increased by more than 30 percent.[44]

This shift from academic to industrial residency programs at the same time that industry is motivated to expand industrial health programs is innovative. Since the professions gain legitimacy and maintain legal monopolies, in large part, through their elite educational systems, control over professional education is an important part of the process. Thus the growth of alternative forms of industrial medicine is accompanied by the attempt to alter professional education to comply with these new legally sanctioned needs. Changes in education thus provide new legally sanctioned monopolies to fulfill legally created needs.

Historically, occupational medicine has been an unpopular specialty, held in low esteem by both workers and the medical establishment. Industry recognized early the need to raise the status of occupational medicine as a specialty and to establish the professionalism of the occupational physician (that is, the physicians' compe-

tence and their claims for independence from corporate manipulation). Saul Kilstein, assistant director of the WBGH during the
1970's, acknowledged that a lot of effort would be required to establish occupational medicine's "credibility and ethical standards"
because it is widely believed "that the occupational medical establishment withholds information and may even manipulate it."[45]

The Series itself depicts occupational medicine as "part of industry's preventive apparatus to mitigate potential losses" under the
workers' compensation program. It acknowledges the common perception that it is precisely because occupational medicine has played
this role historically that it has not been able to establish itself, either
professionally or in popular opinion, as a fully respectable medical
specialty.[46] Nevertheless, the low status of occupational physicians
is blamed upon the low caliber of professionals themselves, their inadequate training programs, and the limited scope of occupational
medicine. The Series identifies the problems of occupational medicine with its isolation from general practice. It holds the AMA responsible for this isolation, for its insistence on distinguishing between health problems that are job related and those that are not.
This insistence is depicted as being based upon attempts by private
physicians to protect their "economic and marketing rights" from
competition by occupational physicians.[47]

Thus the Series attempts to define the problems of occupational
medicine as rooted entirely in the monopolistic practices of physicians themselves. Comments by G. H. Collings, Jr., M.D., head of
New York Telephone's industrial health program, literally transform disability litigation into a squabble between medical specialists, suggesting that litigation occurs in order to determine whether
occupational medicine was impinging on the private practice of
physicians.[48] The fact that industry has a vested interest in defining
any given illness as non-occupational as a fundamental technique for
keeping down workers' compensation costs is never discussed.

Comments by occupational physicians quoted in the Series indicate that they, too, perceive opposition from private practitioners
to be a source of trouble. However, they believe that the boundaries between occupational and private practice are being redrawn.
As evidence for this belief they point out that in the past virtually
no disability was defined as work-related; now virtually all are.[49]

This definitional shift is necessary for industry in the OSHA era because it now stands to minimize its costs under two different circumstances; when either no health problems are defined as work-related or when most of them are. This is obviously true when almost nothing is acknowledged as occupationally caused. It is also true when the damage is seen as so extensive that it becomes a kind of global problem, something that is important to the society as a whole to work out. If the extent of occupationally caused disease is vast enough, the costs can sometimes be passed on to the public, especially if the social value of the industry is thought to be very great or if the economic loss to a particular industry might affect the larger economy.

For example, since passage of the Coal Mine Health and Safety Act of 1969 the cost of the black lung program has been more than $1 billion annually, twenty times the amount paid out to all other workers for work-related diseases. In fact "95 percent of occupational disease benefits in the United States are paid to coalminers and their families."[50] Because coal is an important energy source, and because the costs of benefits are so enormous, the coal industry and the federal government have engaged in both negotiation and litigation to determine financial responsibility. The federal government has paid most of the bill.[51]

The beauties of this technique for passing on the costs of occupational disease were not lost on the asbestos industry, which tried the same strategy unsuccessfully.

It is now in industry's interest to eliminate the boundaries between occupational and non-occupational illness. Because these boundaries have historically been legitimated and maintained by professionals, their elimination entails, at the professional level, some redefinition of the professionals themselves. Occupational physicians must now be evaluated in terms of their ability to do general practice; general practitioners, in terms of their capacities to diagnose and treat work-related illness. One of industry's strategies for accomplishing this redefinition is to attack the historic status superiority of private practitioners by maintaining that they are not, at present, competently trained to handle work-related illness and that their "incentive system" does not dispose them to do it.

Arthur E. Gass, an industrial hygienist with OSHA, asserts that the private physician does not know enough toxicology to ask patients what they are exposed to on their jobs or to evaluate the information if they had it. Gass blames this ignorance on the fact that only about 5 percent of the country's medical schools require any training in toxicology.[52] The Series depicts private practitioners as "excessively conservative" because they keep workers off the job for unnecessarily long periods of time.[53]

Some industrial health practitioners use managerial terminology rather than either medical terminology or the language of professionalism. This usage blurs status distinctions and undermines the historic prestige and monopolies enjoyed by physicians. An extreme example of this use of managerial terminology and organization to replace medical counterparts is provided by the health care management (HCM) program run by G. H. Collings, Jr., M.D., at New York Telephone.[54]

For professional titles, HCM substitutes the terms Level I, Level II, and Level III managers. Level I managers deal with employees who are "deviating" from their customary norms. This means "ill" in traditional terminology. These employees are not "treated" but are "managed" until they return to their "norm."[55] Level II managers plan long-term health "strategies" for employees. These include health education, periodic health monitoring, and the application of preventive measures. Level III managers categorize employees into population groups and subgroups and apply principles of epidemiology and biostatistics to identify procedures that they believe will prove most effective in the prevention of disease.

Each of these managerial levels functions in close interaction with the other two. For example, Level III managers accumulate vast amounts of computerized information that is the foundation for the long-term health stratagems planned by Level II managers. Collings believes that in the future Level III managers might be able to provide computers with enough such information that they can increasingly take over the functions of Level II managers. This process is reminiscent of Braverman's description of the degradation of work, through which skilled tasks are increasingly divided, specialized, supervised, and automated.[56]

The HCM concept requires that a minimum of diagnosis and treatment of illness be done by Level I managers, although Collings states that a certain amount of "laying on of hands" is required in order to "capture" the employee. As soon as possible, however, the employee should be referred to an outside practitioner. Although the employee is referred, she or he is not forgotten. The manager attempts to act as an overseer of the private practitioner who actually treats these employee-patients. Collings acknowledges that some physicians will be unwilling to go along with such supervision, but stresses that managers should not arrive at this conclusion too soon. The Level I manager is "practicing a new art—the art of the practice of Level I management." In that capacity, the manager commands several valuable resources that can make the cooperation of private practitioners an attractive option. These resources include use of the industrial health facility itself to provide the community practitioner with free lab tests, X-rays, electrocardiograms, and any other testing procedures that are available in-house and to do periodic monitoring of common chronic conditions that often fail to interest private practitioners. The results of all these procedures are then reported back to the private physician.

The fact that these tests and procedures are done in-house also means, of course, that the Level I manager has empirical evidence upon which to base peer review of the private practitioners' treatment decisions. Thus Level I managers utilize peer pressure as well as the rewards of affiliation with a rich corporation to motivate the cooperation of private practice physicians. These are the primary techniques for practicing the "art" of management.

Reflected throughout these descriptions of managerial arrangements is an attempt by HCM to eliminate the language of illness and substitute new, non-emotional terms to describe physician services. HCM refers to the procedures followed by managers at all three levels as "units of management," which it has labeled "monads." At Level I these monads are relatively easy to name and identify, because they look and sound pretty much like the descriptors of disease and illness familiar to traditional physicians. However, such terminology is not generally appropriate to describe the functions of other levels of management. For that reason, Collings states, private physicians, who do not usually think of their services as management functions, often find the monad concept difficult to grasp.

One of the purposes of these linguistic transformations is to democratize professional work. Either nurses or physicians may practice Level II management and utilize the same managerial title.

This alteration of the languages of professional status and illness functions at several levels to achieve industry's goals. It demystifies medical practice and professional status claims by depersonalizing illness and converting treatment decisions to mechanical processes based on statistical norms rather than professional judgement. Once the basic assumptions contained within this language are accepted, the physician is no longer even the most logical health care provider. He or she can easily be replaced with a computer or, more likely, a nurse. In fact, the Series often describes nurses as better equipped than physicians to work in industrial clinics. Many corporations utilize nurse-practitioners at very high levels, as heads of their facilities. For example, in Boston nurses are in charge of both Gillette's South Boston facility and the Prudential facility.[57] This use of lower-status personnel to deliver and manage health care services serves the double function of cutting costs immediately and of further undermining control of the health care system by professionals.

SUMMARY

Historically, industry has minimized its liability for work-related disease and injuries through support for certain legislation, such as the workers' compensation laws, control of occupational safety and health data, research funding policies, and the aid of occupational physicians to serve a legitimating function. Industry's structural support network has included legal and political institutions, scientific research, and high-status professionals. Industry continues to use the same sorts of processes to minimize the cost of federal regulations enacted during the last decade.

Despite its numerous complaints, industry does not oppose government regulation per se, particularly regulation of professionals. Even unfriendly regulation, Goldbeck points out, can often be turned to industry's advantage, making government more an ally than an enemy.[58] Industry understands that it can turn regulation to its own advantage bacause government cannot implement laws, regulations, and programs without cooperation from those most directly affected by them in the private sector.[59]

This friendly attitude between government and those regulated by it is analogous to the interaction between physicians and government in the early days of establishing peer review. Peer review could not have been achieved without the cooperation of physicians, who ultimately ended up in control of the system. By the same token, industry has historically controlled occupational safety and health and believes it can use regulations to maintain that control.

The use by government of professional medical expertise to attack rather than to legitimize industrial safety and health practices represents a potential loss of control by industry of an important part of its support network. This threat is intensified by regulations that require industry to relinquish crucial data.

Industry understands the power of this kind of data and the danger inherent in its collection and forced disclosure. The process is the exact reverse of its own attempts to force health care providers to collect and share data on the outcomes of treatment and diagnostic procedures, which would demonstrate the inadequacies of the providers themselves. Only the motivation is different.

Despite the threat, industry is eager to compile a data base for reasons of its own: to demonstrate alleged ineffectuality of or abuse by present providers; to use as evidence that the workers' genetic heritage, not work conditions, is responsible for disease; and, hopefully, to demonstrate that some diseases are not work-related. This compilation requires a new kind of professional to staff the actual operation of data collection and analysis and to interpret the results in industry's interests.

These are all important reasons why industry has undertaken the expansion of industrial health programs. Not all corporations, however, find such activities feasible. The Series points out other alternatives for those who can be persuaded to become actively involved in the health care delivery process. Health maintenance organizations, the topic of the next chapter, provide one of the most practical possibilities.

4

Health Maintenance Organizations

Health maintenance organizations (HMOs) were industry's first strategy for restructuring health care delivery.[1] HMOs are relatively large and complicated delivery systems that utilize greater administrative and managerial sophistication than physicians have previously employed in their routine office practices. As a result of their structure of payments, HMOs lose money if they overutilize patient services. For that reason, they have an economic incentive to limit the services they deliver, just as physicians in traditional practice have an incentive to expand them. So although in theory HMOs provide unlimited services, in practice they embody numerous mechanisms to ration the treatment and diagnostic procedures provided by individual physicians.[2]

For the past fifteen years both government and industry have actively promoted a health maintenance strategy based on the assumption that HMOs can be developed as an alternative to the traditional health care system. Because HMOs deliver services more cost-efficiently than do fee-for-service practices, if a large number of these were developed, the health maintenance strategists predict, they would put so much competitive pressure on the traditional health care system that it would be forced to become more efficient in order to survive.

DEFINITION AND STRUCTURE OF HMOs

HMOs are defined by five essential components, all of which must be present: they are (1) organized systems that provide comprehensive health care services to a consumer population that is (2) voluntarily enrolled. These enrollees are guaranteed (3) a defined set of benefits in return for (4) a prepaid fee that is (5) fixed by contract regardless of the number of services utilized. The contract covers a specified period, usually a year.[3]

Although HMOs are serviced by physicians working in groups, they are far more complex structures than group medical practices. Group practices do not by definition utilize prepayment, enrollment of members, defined benefit schedules, or fixed rates. Conversely, physicians who service HMOs do not necessarily share equipment or technical personnel, as do group practitioners.

Individual physicians working within HMOs may be reimbursed in one of several ways; this is what defines the HMO type. Staff-model HMOs hire physicians and pay them a salary, just as they do any other employee. Prepaid group practice-model HMOs contract with physician or corporate groups to provide all services for a set fee. The best-known HMO of this type is the Kaiser Foundation Health Plan. It contracts with physicians' groups, such as the Southern California Permanente Medical Group, to provide medical services to its enrollees.

These two models are called closed-panel HMOs; this means that physicians on the panels are not paid on the basis of the volume of services they provide but are salaried or otherwise reimbursed as members of the corporate group.

On the other hand, physicians may form groups called independent practice association HMOs and agree to service enrolled members on a fee-for-service basis in their own offices along with their private patients. However, fees for group members, unlike those of the physicians' private patients, are fixed by contract. This is an open-panel HMO.

Only these three models were legally qualified for assistance from the federal government under the Health Maintenance Organization Act of 1973, described below. (This funding was discontinued by the Reagan administration in 1983, but it was an important structural support for ten years.) There exist many other "nonqualified" models that have been supported by industry because they are easier to establish or are more competitive with traditional care than are qualified HMOs, which must comply with the regulations of the HMO Act. Frank Finkenberg of George B. Buck, Consulting Actuaries, warns that compliance with either the HMO Act or its regulations may be against the interests of business, which aims at the creation of competitive HMOs.[4]

Philip Lescohier of William Mercer, Inc., believes that independent practice assocation HMOs (IPA-HMOs), sponsored by businesses, medical foundations, county medical societies, hospitals, and varied combinations of these groups, are more likely than closed-panel types to increase the cost-efficiency of medical care delivery.[5]

Physicians who service all types of HMOs have in common the fact that they share the economic risk of illness with the patient. If they deliver more services than those that would be covered by the fixed fee they are paid, they must absorb the loss. This means they must both submit to peer and utilization review as a condition of the economic survival of the plan and give up their freedom to set their own rates. Thus the HMOs have built into their structures the two major components through which government and industry have attempted to control physician behavior—peer review and economic sanctions.

Bynum Tudor of R. J. Reynolds describes the many kinds of control that corporations can exercise when they own their own HMOs, as Reynolds does: "You have your own utilization review, your own quality control, your own data system built in. You have control of the costs and the services, you have a communication vehicle with the beneficiaries of your health insurance—in short, you have the whole ball of wax."[6]

But Jacob Spies of Employers Insurance of Wausau does not agree that the employer has everything. He complains that employers are not free to offer their employees exactly what they want. Instead, "the services offered are largely controlled by the physicians rather than by. . . . the employer." However, Spies describes the control capabilities of peer and utilization review in terms very similar to those of Damm and Kaplan.[7] Although at Wausau peer review has been developed primarily for ambulatory patients, hospitalization is seen as a very important issue in cost containment policies and is stringently controlled through a concurrent review process. The necessity of all admissions must be certified. Physicians who wish to extend their patients' hospital stays must explain their reasons in writing to a "patient care coordinator," who administers the procedures of the certification process and reports to the physician peer review committee. A physician who does not adhere to these procedures "could end up, after three interim steps, in having the cost of an unauthorized hospital charge deducted from his next payment." The "productivity" of each individual physician is carefully monitored and publicly disclosed by means of a monthly summary report detailing how many patients were seen, what were the average charges, how many services were delivered to each patient, on the average, and how many office visits, hospital visits, and X-rays each physician delivered. Spies notes that some physicians have made "voluntary" changes as a result of these monthly reports. He cites therapeutic injections and office callbacks as two areas in which significant changes have taken place.

Spies' description is of a closed system that reflects virtually every cost containment initiative espoused by industry and in which professionals are controlled to an extent never approached by government regulation. As a result, physicians have changed the substantive practice of medicine in at least one case, therapeutic injections. In spite of these facts, Spies reports that "one hundred percent of the physicians in Wausau are participating in the North Central Health Protection Plan." The same is true in Chippewa Falls and Eau Claire. In Green Bay all but a few physicians have signed the contract, as have over 80 percent of the primary care physicians in Milwaukee. These are impressive figures, given the opposition that physicians have shown in the past to both the HMO concept and controls in general. One reason for this acceptance may be pressure from patients. Wausau publishes a list of participating physicians for its employees, which, Spies says, influenced some physicians to join the plan, after they were contacted by a number of patients asking whether they expected to do so.[8] This is probably a major factor, given that over 94 percent of eligible employees of Wausau have chosen the plan.

In addition to the control inherent in the formal structure of HMOs, other informal mechanisms exist that regulate both organizational practices and client behavior. Mechanic maintains that no health delivery system can survive without some kind of "rationing" mechanism.[9] Prohibitive fees protect traditional practitioners from being overwhelmed by their patients. Because HMOs are service organizations, rather than payment systems, there are no fees to discourage people from using their services. Since the demands of patients are presumed to be infinite, HMOs must use other means to limit utilization. As it happens, this is not a problem at all. The structure of the HMO itself functions simultaneously to maximize utilization control, to ration health care services, and to subordinate physicians to administrative decision making. Mechanic describes the process in detail.

First, it is HMO policy to maintain a tight bed supply. This is an administrative decision designed to reduce the hospitalization of patients. Although advocates of the HMOs claim they eliminate only unnecessary beds that an irrational incentive system has brought into being, this obscures the fact that the rational planning inherent in HMO creation and management is based on a number of goals other than that of maximizing patient health. The most important of these goals is the cost-efficiency that motivated its development in the first place.

Second, HMOs limit out-patient demand in three ways: (1) they control resources made available, such as facilities and personnel, and the geographical distances members must travel to reach them; (2) their review procedures and economic incentives function to make "gatekeepers" of physicians (they withhold referrals to more expensive services) or cause them to limit the extent to which they use more services themselves, such as diagnostic tests, follow-up visits, and so on; and (3) they provide "bureaucratic barriers" designed to make members pay a "non-economic" price for treatment. These barriers include red tape, long waits for both appointments and for walk-in visits, and inaccessibility of physicians for telephone calls.[10]

Although HMO spokespeople usually deny that waiting is a deliberate strategy designed to discourage use, "the Group Health Association, Washington, D.C.'s largest Health Maintenance Organization, has conceded that lengthy appointment delays are intentional to keep down costs."[11] Cost-efficiency is so open a goal of HMOs that one would expect to encounter this kind of frankness with increasing frequency. Some groups are more subject to bureaucratic barriers than others. Mechanic cites findings by Hetherington et al. that the "large prepaid group they studied gave relatively more physician services to the affluent client." High-status, well-educated patients find ways to "play the system, to make demands, to insist on services, to accept "no-nonsense." This suggests that the assertion of HMO advocates that only unnecessary services are eliminated is not true. It is simply used "as a rationalization to tolerate unacceptable practices."[12]

Mechanic also rejects the idea that HMOs are economical because they substitute ambulatory for in-patient care; managers may restrict access to ambulatory as well as hospital care in order to save money. As evidence that they do, he cites a study by Roemer and Shonick that showed that Blue Cross and Blue Shield plans studied delivered 3,984 ambulatory doctor visits per 1,000 persons each year while in group practice the comparable figure was 3,324. Furthermore, even if HMOs did provide more out-patient services, hospital utilization would not be reduced, since almost every study that has been done shows that both out-patient and hospital utilization rates increase slightly when ambulatory services are extended.[13]

These rationing mechanisms provide one good explanation for why HMOs have not proliferated. They have not been popular with the general public. Given a choice, most people prefer to see their own fee-for-service physicians.

HISTORY OF HMO DEVELOPMENT

HMOs have had a long history and a variety of sponsors, including physicians, medical societies, consumer groups, industry, units of government, universities, and medical schools. Each group has been interested in sponsorship as a response to events in the larger health care environment.

Drs. Donald E. Ross and H. Clifford Loos started the first prepaid medical practice in the United States in 1929, while simultaneously maintaining thriving surgical practices. Their membership consisted of the fifteen hundred employees of the Los Angeles Department of Water and Power. Despite strong opposition from their county medical society, which attempted to expel them in 1934, the Ross-Loos plan enrolled many other groups of city employees without difficulty.[14] By 1973 the plan had 120,000 prepaid patients, 150 physicians, 10 satellite offices, and a 152-bed medical center.[15]

The depression saw a resurgence of social movements around health care issues[16] that contributed to the development of HMOs by consumer groups.[17] For example, the first urban consumer plan, Group Health Association of Washington, D.C., became operational in 1937. It was sponsored by employees of the Home Owners' Loan Corporation and is now one of the six largest plans in the country.

The federal government both stimulated and helped subsidize the largest and most successful prepaid plan in the country, the Kaiser Foundation Health Plan, as a side effect of funding huge construction projects in remote areas lacking health care facilities for workers. The Kaiser plan began at the construction sites of the Hoover, Grand Coulee, and Bonneville dams, which Kaiser Industries built under government contracts during the 1930's. During the 1940's, Kaiser Industries shifted from dam to ship construction and built clinics for its shipyard workers in Oakland, Richmond, and Vancouver and for its mine workers in Fontana, California. These clinics, which were recognized by the authorities as a legitimate operating expense, were financed by government contracts. After the war these clinics and their equipment were declared surplus war property. Kaiser bought them at 1 percent of cost through the Kaiser Hospital Foundation, which was established for that purpose.[18] Now "the king of the HMO mountain," the Kaiser plan has 36 percent of the nation's HMO population—4.3 million members. In 1982 its revenues reached $2.4 billion.[19]

Local governments have also contributed to HMO development. In 1947 the City of New York became the first unit of government to sponsor a prepaid group practice, the Health Insurance Plan of Greater New York (HIP).

Throughout this process, of course, organized medicine opposed HMO development.[20] In 1943 the U.S. Supreme Court ruled that the District of Columbia Medical Society, prompted by the AMA, conspired to deny Medical Society membership to HMO-related physicians, making it impossible for them to obtain hospital staff privileges.[21] In 1951 a Seattle, Washington, medical society and a hospital were found liable under state anti-trust laws for conspiring to deny hospital privileges to HMO physicians.[22] And as late as the 1970's the Federal Trade Commission (FTC) obtained consent orders in two cases involving alleged discrimination against HMO-affiliated physicians. One in 1976 prohibited a Blue Shield Plan in Spokane, Washington, from treating unfavorably physicians who served HMO subscribers. The other was issued in 1979 and prohibited an organization in Pittsburgh from conspiring to exclude HMO-affiliated physicians from its medical staffs.[23]

Although organized medicine opposed HMO development in general, in 1954 it responded with its own version of prepaid care, one that has been acceptable to at least part of the physician community. That year the first foundation for medical care in the United States was organized by the San Joaquin County Medical Society.[24] Its purpose was to establish a plan to "provide comprehensive health services on a prepaid, fixed-fee basis to labor groups dissatisfied with their previous medical care arrangements."[25] All members of the medical society who were in private practice were permitted to participate in the plan. Although these foundations continued to develop, their numbers were small until the 1960's, when they were rejuvenated by medical societies in an attempt to keep peer review in professional hands.[26]

Industry has been able to use the foundations well by hiring them to establish both PSROs and HMOs. Conversely, this support by corporations stimulated development of two professional organizations, the American Association of Foundations for Medical Care (AAFMC) and the American Association of Professional Service Review Organizations (AAPSRO).[27] These once minor organizational forms then were available to government and industry as bases upon which to organize and legitimate peer and utilization review in the 1960's after the passage of industry-supported PSRO legislation. Except for closed-panel HMO organizations, which have always been unpopular among physicians, these foundations have been the only physicians' groups through which health plans could be set up.[28] The Series predicted early that they would be an important force for establishing independent practice association HMOs and, thus, for forcing changes in the traditional health care system. This has proven to be the case.

During the 1960's and 1970's medical schools, universities, and insurance carriers became involved with HMO development for the first time.[29] The Harvard Medical School and Washington University plans became operational in 1969 and the Rush Medical School and Yale University plans in 1971.[30] *Business Week* reported in May

1977 that twenty-two insurance companies were involved in 50 HMOs in twenty-five states. The Blue Cross and Blue Shield associations were sponsors, administrators, or promoters and marketers of 107 HMOs.

The business community has shown active interest in HMO development since the early 1970's. Articles in *Fortune*, *Forbes*, *Business Week*, and the *Wall Street Journal* have advocated HMO development.[31] During the same period representatives of the federal government began making their first public announcements in favor of HMOs, at first for Medicaid and Medicare patients and then for private patients as well.

Historically, the HMO concept has been of interest to large numbers of diverse and powerful groups. The idea and some very successful prototypes have been around for decades. Why has the HMO option been so slow to develop? Opposition by the medical profession is one obvious and easy explanation. Physicians and their professional associations have actively and conspicuously fought HMO development, as for example the Ross-Loos plan discussed above. They have also used their influence and lobbying power to obtain certain state laws and regulations that have functioned as barriers to HMO development and operation. The most effective of these have been prohibitions against the "corporate" practice of medicine (the selling of physician services by non-physicians) and the so-called Blue Shield laws, which have helped maintain medical society control over service plans by guaranteeing the societies' control of the governing boards of all HMOs in their areas and requiring that all physicians in the area be eligible to deliver services through the plans. They thus eliminate the sanctioning power of peer review. Another common state law that has prevented the successful marketing of HMOs has been the prohibition of professional advertising; HMOs have thus been prevented from soliciting members by advertising services, charges, or other non-professional features of their operation. These obstacles have been under attack from two directions since the mid–1970's. The first was from the HMO Act itself and the second from more general legal processes, such as application by the Federal Trade Commission of Sherman anti-trust laws to the health care sector. These processes will be discussed below.

Professional opposition, supported by state laws and regulations, is of course, part of the explanation for the fact that prepaid group plans have not been the dominant health care delivery structure in this country. This cannot be the whole story, however. One essential fact remains unexplained. In certain times and places, despite opposition from physicians, HMOs have developed and flourished; and the legal system, rather than supporting the professional monopoly, has been directed against it. Municipal, state, and even federal governments have all supported successful HMOs, despite the AMA's legendary lobbying power.

When other conditions are conducive to HMO development, professional opposition seems almost irrelevant. That being the case, why did physicians control legislation in their own interest until the early 1970's without interference? Possibly because no one particularly cared. Until that time, no large powerful group had been sufficiently interested to push for HMO development except in isolated, local areas, where their efforts were often successful. HMOs cost a lot of money to start up. No one advocated spending such sums to duplicate existing health care delivery facilities until health care costs became a national topic. Industry did not begin to protest increased health care costs until the late 1960's, when inflation in the health care sector soared, largely as a result of passage of Medicare and Medicaid. Within four years, the health maintenance strategy had emerged. Once industry became interested in cutting its own costs, the development of HMOs as an alternative to traditional medical practice became a serious possibility, since they were, from the beginning, the heart of industry's restructuring strategy.

THE "HEALTH MAINTENANCE STRATEGY"

The development of the health maintenance strategy is generally credited to Paul M. Ellwood, M.D., who described it in a position paper submitted to President Nixon in 1970.[32] Ellwood is president of InterStudy, an organization specializing in human services policy research. He was a key health consultant to President Nixon and to both houses of Congress, and he has worked continuously with large corporations, urging them to convert corporate medical department into profit-making HMOs. Ellwood is an active participant in Center for Industry and Health Care conferences and publications, where his work is often cited. He is widely published, cited, and interviewed in both the business and health provider press as a leading expert in medical economics. His strategy includes the following components.

First, the federal government should stop attempting to regulate and plan the health care system. It should focus instead on legislation that would provide economic subsidies for HMO development. It should also eliminate restrictive state legislation, such as bans on professional advertising. These actions would stimulate the emergence of a "self-regulating" health maintenance industry. Second, preventive medical practice should be emphasized. The traditional system rewards providers for treating illness; HMOs reward them for preventing it. Third, ambulatory care should be substituted for expensive hospital in-patient care. Fourth, health care should be integrated and coordinated (that is, rationalized) to embody the same efficiencies as the corporate world. Ellwood envisioned a complex system of about one thousand HMOs throughout the country, which would be organized like large corporations and could service several million people each.[33]

HMOs, as a powerful competitor in the medical marketplace, would thus force a transformation in the less efficient, traditional system with its irrational incentives, which inevitably results in overutilization at all levels in the health care system. Ellwood's strategy would draw heavily on government authority and business efficiency, both of which are bureaucratically structured, to revamp the traditional, professionally dominated system in the interest of cutting costs.

In keeping with the recommendations in Ellwood's position paper, HEW Secretary Robert H. Finch announced in a press release on March 25, 1970, that legislation would be introduced authorizing the Social Security Administration to contract with HMOs to guarantee "comprehensive health services for the elderly (and poor) at a fixed annual rate. . . . State Medicaid programs would also be permitted to contract with HMOs for Medicaid recipients."[34]

Although the federal government first proposed legislative support for HMOs for Medicare and Medicaid patients, as it had earlier mandated peer review for the same groups, that support was soon extended to the private sector, again as with peer review. On

February 18, 1971, President Nixon's Health Message to Congress described HMOs as a proven system upon which a national health strategy was to be built for all segments of the population.[35]

For the next three years, organized medicine successfully attempted to move the administration away from its strong support for HMOs. When the HMO Act was finally signed into law on December 29, 1973, industry was not happy with the results. According to the Series, the economic incentives designed to stimulate HMO development were crippled because their qualification requirements were unreasonably stringent, the result of a political alliance between conservative forces in organized medicine and liberal forces seeking to make HMOs a "panacea."[36]

In analyzing the HMO Act, Birnbaum differentiates between its "favorable" and "potentially detrimental" provisions.[37] In the favorable spectrum he includes, first, authorization of government grants, loans, and loan guarantees to establish new HMOs and expand existing ones. This is extremely important, since start-up costs for new HMOs were prohibitive for many groups. In 1974, when the HMO Act was first being implemented, the minimum capital investment for construction of a central clinical facility was $2 million. Furthermore, the new HMO would operate at a deficit until membership reached a break-even point, which could take as long as five years. This fact provides another good explanation for why HMOs have not proliferated.

The second favorable provision Birnbaum lists is the dual-choice mandate, which requires employers who are subject to minimum wage laws and employ twenty-five or more persons to offer HMO membership to their employees if a qualified HMO is in operation in the area. "Qualified" is defined as meeting the regulatory requirements of the HMO Act.

Third, the act preempted state laws and regulations that have functioned as barriers to HMO development and operation, such as the Blue Shield laws and bans on professional advertising mentioned above.

Industry supports all these provisions but abhors the regulations attached to them. In order to obtain the grants or loans, to be offered as a dual-choice option, to avoid physician control, and to advertise its services, an HMO must meet these standards, which constitute part of what Birnbaum calls the "potentially detrimental provision," of the HMO Act.

The first of these was the requirement that a qualified HMO offer a more comprehensive range of basic health services than do indemnity plans or already established HMOs. These services included short-term mental health services and preventive dental care for children.

Second, qualified HMOs were required to conduct "open enrollment" periods each year, during which time non-group enrollees from the community at large must be accepted on a first-come-first-served basis. These open enrollment individuals would certainly include disproportionate numbers with medical problems that may have kept them from obtaining insurance coverage in the private marketplace.

Third, it required that all members, including those individually enrolled, pay a fee that is "community-rated" as opposed to "experience-rated," thus forcing the HMO to perform the kind of community service that once put Blue Cross and Blue Shield at such a competitive disadvantage.

Fourth, the act required that at least a third of the plan's governing body be enrolled members. This would benefit community-based HMOs but would cause great troubles for those that are corporate-based and whose members are employees.

Fifth, the act provided that HEW continue to regulate qualified HMOs that utilized its financial assistance or dual-choice options. Regulations would be enforced through civil court action if other means of securing compliance failed.

These regulations were the antithesis of industry's aim, which was to recreate the health care system into a free market institution in which competition and the profit motive would simultaneously make health care more cost-efficient and provide large numbers of people with high-quality health care. Free market advocates maintain that quality care will follow from rationalization and cost-efficiency under competition, not regulation. The regulations, they argue, will reduce the quality of care by limiting rationalization.

The first four of these five regulations are reflections more of liberal attempts to ensure that HMOs would be of service to the community than of professional obstructionism. Again, the ability of physicians to influence legislation enactments is contingent on support from other important forces in the social environment. But industry's strategy does not focus on liberal coalitions, which come and go. The professional monopoly remains the permanent target.

The relationship between the costs of services and the quality of care is a big issue in health maintenance strategy. Advocates and critics alike claim that HMOs reduce health care costs; they disagree about how those reductions are achieved. The Conference Board cites an actuarial analysis that attributes savings to reduced hospital utilization among HMO enrollees and to organizational efficiencies. However, the board states these advantages will accrue only on the condition that the practice of preventive medicine successfully averts higher subsequent costs.[38]

The preventive medicine argument provides an example of changes in the theories of HMO advocates during the past fifteen years. In the beginning HMOs attempted to practice preventive medicine; they recommended and delivered periodic physical examinations and screening procedures in the expectation that detecting pathologies early would make them less expensive to treat. The belief in preventive medicine was based upon common sense, as no data existed through which it could be tested. Nevertheless, HMOs were promoted largely on the basis of that theory. Ironically, the HMOs then collected data that were used to *disprove* the theory that screenings were cost-efficient or that they actually reduce mortality or morbidity statistics.

Physicians are now reconsidering a formerly hallowed concept, the preventive value of an annual physical examination.

Concern over the value of and benefit to the patient of such routine periodic examinations coupled with the ever increasing costs of health care have combined to force reconsideration of the entire concept. Cost benefit analysis is becoming an integral part of any discussion about health care. Controlled studies have demonstrated no difference in morbidity or mortality between screened and unscreened populations.[39]

Having used the preventive medicine argument to get started, HMOs have abandoned it because it was too expensive and, apparently, because it was untrue. The original procedure was to be universal screening, which, because it delivered services to massive numbers of people, required more sophisticated administrative management and made multi-specialty group practices and use of paraprofessional personnel very functional. Salmon describes a process analogous to factory production. HMOs could compete with traditional practitioners by "conversion to larger units of production, technological innovation, division of labor, substitution of capital for labor."[40]

This is, of course, the process of industrialization of health care, with a concomitant degradation and dilution of professional work. Once these mass-produced services were initially rationalized, however, managers noticed that screening services are very expensive. They concluded they are not cost-efficient. Additional economies must be achieved through increased rationalization, using the computer to determine when an individual is in need of screening, on the basis of statistical probability. This is an extension of the experience-rating (as opposed to community-rating) concept as applied to physical examinations. Instead of sharing the costs among the entire group to screen even low-risk members, cost analysis is done that assigns each individual to a rating group in which the cost-effectiveness of screening him or her is then evaluated. Thus G. H. Collings, Jr., M.D., of New York Telephone, determines that pap smears for young women employees of the telephone company are not cost-efficient, even done in-house, because of the low incidence of cancer. Each cancer detected in this group would cost about a quarter of a million dollars. It is cheaper to treat the cancer. The *New York Times* reports a poignant example of the human outcome of this philosophy through an interview with a thirty-one-year-old Kaiser plan patient dying of stomach cancer. When he first presented himself at the Kaiser facility with stomach pains at the age of twenty-nine, he was given an X-ray but not a probe with a gastroscope, which later detected the cancer, because, the chief surgeon said, there was no reason to suspect cancer in someone that young.[41] The philosophy that mass screenings of symptom-free populations should be discontinued on the basis of statistical data is extended to the treatment of patients presenting symptoms.

In sum, alternative health care systems legitimated themselves partly on the grounds that they provided services defined by physicians as good preventive medicine—annual examinations—to great numbers of people. Once established, they withdrew the service and, in the process, stimulated physicians to redefine good preventive med-

icine on the basis of cost-efficiency. Bureaucratic rationalization altered the substantive practice of medicine not only through overt
controls but also through the redefinition of the operative reality, a
process that is both painless and invisible. Physician acceptance then
legitimated a bureaucratic decision based upon cost-efficiency.

There are other interesting variations in definitions of preventive
medicine. Industry emphasizes personal behavior, lifestyle intervention, and initiatives in health education in the areas of nutrition,
smoking, and alcoholism. It also favors immunizations and screening for hypertension, diabetes, and other major killers that can be
controlled to some extent with patient cooperation. Industry opposes screenings that are perceived as threatening to itself, however,
in particular those designed to detect occupationally caused illness.
In opposing such screenings, Goldbeck says:

the Toxic Substances Control Act alone will require over 20 million workers to be screened at least annually. The number of medical problems discovered quite apart from those the tests were designed to identify, will be
staggering, and will give rise to numerous questions of responsibility for
follow-up, payment, confidentiality, and so forth.[42]

This is an interesting situation. As noted earlier, screenings have
not been shown, statistically, to reduce morbidity or mortality rates.
However, they do detect pathology and could function to identify
occupational health hazards. Ultimately this could result in reduced
morbidity and mortality if the objective were to eliminate the health
hazard, but that is not the goal of the act. As things stand, the Toxic
Substances Control Act could indict industry without improving our
national health statistics, and that is an argument against the act.

Industry has opposed all regulations designed to carry out such
screening procedures. The coal industry, for example, fought passage of the Coal Mine Health and Safety Act, which requires
screening of workers for black lung disease; it passed in 1969 any-
way. The industry cited, as one reason for its opposition, the fear
that workers would become the victims of iatrogenesis (doctor-caused
disease) if they had that much contact with physicians.[43]

Despite talk by health maintenance strategists about preventive
and high-quality medical services, the major attraction of HMOs
appears to have been their potential for the exercise of external con-

trol over professional services in order to cut costs in the health care sector.

Advocates of HMOs often claim that they are the only viable alternative to federal regulation; they are thus the lesser of two evils. Talk of the suffocating layers of bureaucracy has frightened many once hostile physicians into the HMO camp. The processes of modern management are never described as bureaucratic, although in fact HMO organization has the potential for much more comprehensive control and centralization than that achieved by federal regulations. The national network of HMOs envisioned by Ellwood would regulate health care delivery to an extent never imagined by government bureaucrats. This regulation would be accomplished by private managers rather than government, because the latter sometimes responds to professional interest groups and consumer demands with legislation that industry abhors.

The HMO Act of 1973 provides an example of the kind of regulation industry fears. It attempted to force HMOs to perform public services, such as charging community-rated fees and doing peer review designed to control utilization and assure quality care. HMO advocates complain that these regulations reduce their competitive advantage. They want capitation fees based on experience rating and peer and utilization review that functions in the interest of administrative planning and cost reduction. Both industry and government want to control the health care system; only their objectives are somewhat different.

Like all complex organizations, HMOs may be directed toward a variety of goals, which are largely determined by both the nature of the organization itself and the goals of those who control it. The processes of complex organizations are comparable to those of systematic research methodologies: they are neutral in themselves but are capable of application to many types of problems, including those of interest groups whose goals may or may not be rational.

The goals of HMOs are multiple and are built into the structure and processes of the organization. They include implementing competition; planning on the basis of cost-efficiency; maintaining quality equal to that of traditional medicine; and earning a profit for "someone other than the physician involved," as Professor Clark Havighurst puts it.[44] These goals are seen as desirable in themselves, and additionally they constitute the components of the long-range goal of industry, a transformed health care system. The health maintenance strategy claims that, with certain supportive federal legislation, HMOs will both improve health care and cut its costs by the practice of preventive medicine and the utilization of appropriate settings, that is, out-patient rather than hospital facilities. The capacity to cut costs will make HMOs either so competitive that traditional medicine will be forced to adopt its practices. Yet there is no evidence that HMOs either practice preventive medicine effectively or that they substitute ambulatory for out-patient care. Rather, economies in HMOs appear to be achieved through rationalization procedures aimed at reducing services.

The next section will examine four ways in which industry has attempted to facilitate HMO development and its strategies for dealing with the disincentives of the HMO Act. These include supporting the development of nonqualified HMOs; accepting independent practice association HMOs; pushing for amendments to the HMO Act that will make it less restrictive (that is, regulative); and, finally, supporting the newest form of rationalized practice, preferred provider organizations (PPOs).

NONQUALIFIED HMOs

There were important reasons why an HMO might wish to meet the qualifying regulations of the HMO Act. The classic HMO form, prepaid group practice, is very expensive to start up;[45] many group sponsors must meet federal qualification standards in order to obtain essential funding. Even those groups that have been privately funded may be forced to qualify in order to be offered as a dual-choice option or to advertise and market the HMO.

An example of the problems associated with funding, even when powerful, prestigious institutions are involved, is provided by the Harvard Community Health Plan. The plan was originally financed by loans from Harvard Medical School and by grants from the Commonwealth Fund, Rockefeller Foundation, and Ford Foundation, which totalled $1.5 million. The first center opened in Boston in 1969, five years before the HMO Act provided for federal funding. The plan had marketing problems from the beginning because state legislative requirements forced it to market itself through Blue

Cross and Blue Shield, which performed poorly. The marketing failure by the Blues was attributed to a set of "mixed incentives": they risked no capital, were too conservative for aggressive marketing strategies, and often had to "cannibalize" their own group policies to enroll the HMOs, which then competed with their other plans. In 1977 a new state HMO-enabling act made it possible for the plan to drop its Blue Cross affiliation and contract directly with subscriber groups. Also in 1977 the plan obtained federal qualification and began to expand, doing its own advertising and marketing.[46]

This example indicates that some kinds of HMOs can flourish without either federal funding or the dual-choice options if they can obtain financial support elsewhere. The Series urges industry to assist HMOs to obtain non-federal money.[47] Ronald Kilgren of Ford Motor Company urges business leaders to help new plans to obtain long-term financing from lending institutions, which, he says, will be more inclined to help in developing HMOs if they are actively supported by "established business interest."[48] R. J. Reynolds Industries, Inc., in Winston-Salem, North Carolina, financed its own plan, thus making the greatest commitment to private health care delivery any corporate employer has made since the organization of the Kaiser-Permanente system.[49]

Some kinds of HMOs, such as unqualified multi-specialty group practice HMOs, are inexpensive to establish, so funding is not a problem. These build on one or more group practices that already exist in a community. The groups form a consortium and then each group contracts with the HMO to deliver all medical services to enrolled members. This model is similar to the prepaid group practice HMO except that it also provides fee-for-service for non-HMO members.

Because it consolidates existing practices, this kind of HMO does not require either large investments in new facilities or extensive marketing. In addition, the revenue obtained from the existing fee-for-service practice allows the group to include more physicians and specialties than it otherwise could at absolutely no cost.[50] The fee-for-service private practice thus helps to subsidize development of the prepaid group practice, which aims at the elimination of fee-for-service practice.

By 1977, multi-specialty groups were fairly widespread. Approximately 3,000 were operating in the United States, of which some 375 received prepayment revenue.[51]

Industry's early involvement with developing multi-specialty group practices consisted of support and encouragement, not direct sponsorship, although in some cases the support and encouragement were quite extensive. For example, the business community in Minneapolis established the Twin Cities Health Care Development Project to promote HMO development in the Minneapolis-Saint Paul area. Their efforts were very successful. The Conference Board estimated in 1974 that there would have been only two or three HMOs without the efforts of the project, rather than the eight or ten that were either operating or being planned in the summer of 1973. By 1979 the area had seven prepayment plans, which were credited with reducing hospital admission and utilization rates for Medicare patients.[52]

The Twin Cities project provided technical assistance to groups interested in joining HMOs, provided marketing assistance to new HMOs, and worked with the Minnesota legislature to pass HMO-enabling legislation. As in most other states, the Blue Shield laws were regarded as very restrictive. The project helped gather support for legislation to establish the legality of the new HMOs that were in the process of formation.[53] The legislation did not, however, "allow for-profit HMOs, as the project desired."[54]

In 1976 the project reorganized itself as the National Association of Employers on Health Maintenance Organizations, in order to assist its roughly 120 member companies to sponsor and work with HMOs and to offer employees HMO membership "as an alternative to traditional insurance coverage."[55]

By 1983 about 30 percent of the population of Minneapolis and Saint Paul was enrolled in an HMO—one of the highest rates in the country. According to Gary Appel, President of the Council of Community Hospitals, Minneapolis, the HMOs have forced hospital utilization rates so low that hospitals have an average occupancy of only 65 percent and are "desperate for patients." The HMOs have had exactly the effect in the Twin Cities area that was predicted by health maintenance strategists: as their premium rates go down due to reductions of services, the rates of those insured by other plans have gone up. Blue Cross insurance premiums rose about

20 percent in the area in 1982, while cost increases for HMOs were less than half that rate. The average cost per hospital admission for a member of the Physicians' Health Plan of Minnesota, an IPA-HMO, was $1,600, compared with $3,349 for a Blue Cross enrollee. As a result, Blue Cross has launched a preferred provider organization (PPO), called AWARE, which has resulted in such frantic discounting of rates by hospitals that it is "beginning to have some of the earmarks of a price war."[56]

Preferred provider organizations are the latest development on the group practice front. Unlike IPAs and closed-panel HMOs, they are not prepaid plans. Structurally they function more like IPAs than other group plans. The group may be made up of practicing physicians, or a hospital, with or without its medical staff, or even by a corporation. It agrees to provide services to its members, at a negotiated rate, which is usually 15–20 percent lower than fees for non-members. It can offer these rates because it negotiates discounts from hospitals and because its members usually are selected groups of employed people with low morbidity statistics, although Medicare-eligible groups are also desirable. Payments for the latter are assured and allow higher utilization than is normally delivered by HMOs. PPO members do not have to use preferred providers to get reimbursement, but if they use non-PPOs, they will pay higher deductibles and co-payments.[57] PPO development was supported in California by new state legislation that allowed insurance companies and employers to contract directly with providers. At least 160 PPOs "are now knocking at the doors of major corporations, hoping to nail them to contracts" in California.[58] Thus industry makes use of exactly the same kinds of structural supports in their restructuring strategy that physicians have used to maintain their occupational monopoly—government legislation at the state as well as federal levels.

Industry's legislative activities are often contradictory, in some cases supporting enforcement of anti-trust laws and in other cases opposing them. Support is provided wherever it would remove control of the system from the hands of professionals. For example, Havighurst urges support for the enforcement of anti-trust laws directed against "professional conspiracies" that "have stood in the way of third-party innovations in the past." He believes anti-trust legislation "can put the ball in the private sector's court."[59] In particular, Havighurst supports anti-trust to strengthen the hand of the insurance industry, which he believes will rationalize the health care system if fear of professional retaliation is removed.

All those who support HMOs support anti-trust prosecutions where professional societies restrict their development. This is a major topic in the Series, volume 4, which deals with problems encountered in marketing HMOs because of professional bans on advertising. Such bans have been a major cause of anti-trust actions by the FTC. For example, in 1979 the FTC ruled that the AMA had unlawfully restricted competitive advertising by physicians and ordered it to stop characterizing the use of health maintenance organizations or similar health care delivery plans as unethical. The AMA was also prohibited from labeling "the ownership or management of health care organizations by non-professionals as unethical."[60] This ruling was doubly attractive to industry, since it not only attacked professional attempts to block the development of HMOs but also undermined mechanisms for keeping existing ones in professional hands.

The FTC aimed not only at eliminating professional obstruction of alternative systems but also at "prohibiting physician groups from participating in the control of prepaid health plans or Blue Cross and Blue Shield plans." In 1979 Terry Winslow, Assistant Director of the Bureau of Competition in the FTC, told a group of employers, the Council on Employee Benefits, that there is "less competition in the health care delivery system than one supposes would be the case if there weren't some sort of restraints on the system being imposed by some providers themselves." As a result, Winslow told the group, "many Blue Cross and Blue Shield plans just aren't giving you employers your money's worth."[61]

Industry opposes anti-trust activity when it is directed toward new processes of which industry approves, such as the setting of certain kinds of rates and fees, which is the heart of prepayment plans, or price-setting arrangements such as those between some Blue Shield plans and pharmacies covering prescription drugs. In 1979 the U.S. Supreme Court ruled that the latter were not exempt from anti-trust laws.[62] This kind of anti-trust enforcement directly interferes with rationalization processes, not to mention the lower rates for the same goods and services for group members.

Industry's experiences with HMO development over the past decade have led to some changes in the HMO strategy. More variations are acceptable now than were originally envisioned. Ellwood himself now concedes the need to transform the system in "stages." These stages could take advantage of features of group practices without the major advantages attributed to HMOs, that is, risk sharing and the elimination of fee-for-service. One such stage of development is simply aggregation of physician practices, forming them into groups but not necessarily HMOs: "by aggregating physicians and then experience-rating them, you can create a device with the seeds of continuing change built into it which still has the capacity to contain costs."[63]

This theory holds that when providers are aggregated for pricing purposes—even if in artificial groups—they begin to compete with other groups. This competition causes groups to "police" their membership and exclude physicians "whose wasteful practice patterns inflate the cost of care."[64]

A later stage of aggregation is the group practice, which industry also encourages. In 1975 the Robert Wood Johnson Foundation, which provided funding for the establishment of a data base on independent practice association performance at the Center for Industry and Health Care,[65] announced that it would award grants totalling $30 million to establish up to sixty group practices that were to be based in non-profit hospitals.[66] In 1983 the foundation began giving grants for the development of PPOs. From twelve to twenty planning grants will be given out by 1984. Ten of these grant recipients will be given $1.5 million to implement their plans.[67]

The aggregation theory suggests that any form of grouping can function to control professional workers and that the elaborate administrative apparatus of HMOs may be unnecessary. This appears to be a planned variation on Johnson's theory, under which physicians lose power when their clientele are organized into some kind of large group.[68] In this case it is grouping the physicians themselves, as encouraged by industry, that will result in loss of professional power.

INDEPENDENT PRACTICE ASSOCIATIONS (IPAs)

Although closed-panel prepaid group practices are very costly and difficult to establish, independent practice associations build on existing practices, thus eliminating capital investment and marketing problems. Historically the IPA has been the only model acceptable to organized medicine.

The IPA is more similar to traditional medical practice than staff-model HMOs. It collects fees on a capitation basis, as do other HMOs, thus using prepayment in fixed dollars to control health care costs. But IPAs reimburse physicians on a fee-for-service basis; they do not pay salaries. Thus IPAs can have many physicians available, but unlike staff-model HMOs it has to pay them only for services they actually deliver. Of course, they are paid less for the same services delivered under prepayment agreements than they receive from fee-for-service patients. This model is most likely to be owned and/or controlled by a physician or medical society.

In the beginning IPAs were not popular among HMO advocates, who aimed at the complete elimination of the traditional system. Many of these were concerned that physician-controlled IPAs would not be as cost-efficient as other models. This fear was based on the fact that IPAs did not reduce hospital utilization as effectively as do staff-model HMOs. In the Minneapolis-Saint Paul area, for example, the Minnesota State Department of Health reported in 1979 that for all seven HMOs operating in the area the utilization rate was 548 hospital days per thousand population per year; 720 days for Blue Cross and Blue Shield and private insurance patients; and 639 days in the one IPA operating in the area at that time.[69]

The Center for Industry and Health Care has been particularly interested in IPAs and has been establishing a national data base on IPA performance with the aid of the Robert Wood Johnson Foundation.[70] The Series, which supports development of fee-for-service HMOs, enumerates their disadvantages and their advantages. The disadvantages all involve control of medical practice by physicians. In the beginning physician groups were unwilling to accept certain kinds of HMO controls. For example, because preadmission certification programs represent a dramatic change from traditional practice, fee-for-service HMOs often refused to use them. However, as the Series points out, preadmission certification programs have proven enormously effective in controlling hospital admissions. Plans such as the Physicians' Health Plan of Greater Minneapolis, which at first refused to adopt the programs, had major problems with overutilization. When they found themselves on the brink of bankruptcy, they were forced to implement preadmission certification as an important component of their recovery strategy.[71]

Thus even though IPAs are physician controlled and maintain some traditional features, they must adopt the same kinds of utilization control mechanisms as do other HMOs in order to survive economically. Market mechanisms force physicians to rationalize their own practices, even when they are theoretically in control of their own administrative apparatus. This is, of course, exactly what the HMO strategy predicted in 1970.

IPAs with stringent peer review and risk-sharing mechanisms utilize the same information-gathering procedures as do other HMOs, including the use of computers to generate productivity information and the distribution of monthly reports that summarize the practice patterns of every physician in the group. These summaries are ordered by specialty so their performances can be compared. The reports may name individual physicians or use random identifying numbers. The information they provide includes averages of numbers of visits for each patient, numbers of diagnostic tests per visit, costs to the practice per visit, and total cost for each physician. Such information is a potent mechanism for applying peer pressure. "Practice habits change without anybody saying much of anything!"[72]

IPAs present many advantages to industry. First, as noted above, if it is to survive, the IPA must implement efficient peer and utilization review. To do so requires that a management information system be created. This is being done through the development of sophisticated computer software to provide the relevant information.[73] This management information is of a different category than that used in traditional administrative communications. Its objective is not traditional administrative coordination but the reshaping of physician practice habits. The reports detail practice decisions by physician, including both those who are cited in specific complaints and those whose practice patterns appear to be out of line. On a more general level, peer review committees may also review a random sample of cases in order to identify a number of physicians as overutilizers and then follow up on them. This represents a kind of electronic surveillance.

This is an example of the development by administrators of increasingly fine categorizations. First, gross deviations are singled out and then the deviations within smaller samples. The behavior of physicians can then be modified through sanctioning. Physicians who do not comply may be "terminated"; this sanction has been used by several fee-for-service HMOs.[74]

The second advantage for industry of the IPA model is that it is the one most acceptable to individual physicians. It is thus easier to recruit professional support.

Third, IPAs can be started in almost any community. Since overhead costs are lower than for salaried groups (in part because they are subsidized by the physicians' private practices, as in multi-specialty groups), the break-even population ranges from five thousand to twenty thousand members, whereas for salaried groups it is closer to fifty thousand.

Fourth, IPAs are acceptable to larger numbers of people in the community, since they are not required to change physicians or otherwise change their health care habits to join. These patients then put pressure on their own physicians to participate in the plans, as in the Wausau plan, cited earlier.

Although IPAs are criticized for being physician owned and controlled, industry has been more supportive of them than have non-IPA-HMO professionals. As early as 1974 the Conference Board spoke favorably of fee-for-service HMOs, in discussing the Lovelace Clinic in Albuquerque, New Mexico.[75] The Center for Industry and Health Care has advocated their use since its establishment.

A report prepared for HEW Secretary Califano in 1979 indicated that of the 217 HMOs that were operational at that time, 59.4 percent were group or "staff model" HMOs, 36.9 percent were IPAs, and 3.7 percent were of unknown ownership. However, the report also noted that of 100 private HMOs that were in various stages of development at that time, 52.0 percent were staff models, 40.0 percent were IPAs, and 8.0 percent were of unknown ownership. An additional 82 projects were receiving federal development assistance; 47.7 percent staff models and 51.2 percent IPAs.[76]

Although the percentage of IPAs was growing, the growth of HMOs in general did not approach the predictions of early advocates. When the Nixon administration first announced the HMO strategy in 1971, the goal was the development of 450 by 1973 and 1,700 by 1976; the enrollment aimed at was 40 million. By 1980, HMOs were to be available to 90 percent of the population.[77] However, in July–August 1975 *Group Practice* reported that only three HMOs had qualified for certification since the HMO Act passed in 1973, citing as causes the detrimental regulations described by Birnbaum. Throughout the 1970's both the provider and popular presses reported low growth rates; then, in late 1979, the tone became optimistic. Although the numbers of HMOs were still small, enrollment increases, which were less than 2 percent in 1976, went to 5 percent in 1977 and jumped to 18 percent in 1978.[78] It was at this point that provider interest in IPAs increased.

Countrywide, 270 plans are now treating 11.6 million people. Wherever HMOs have gained a real foothold they have had the competitive impact predicted by industry. Why have they proven so difficult to establish?

HMO LEGISLATION, MARKETING, AND GROWTH RATES

Almost as soon as the HMO Act was signed into law in 1973, a number of interested groups began to push for amendments.[79] Within industry HMO strategists complained loudly that "Congress has very nearly strangled the HMO concept by embracing it."[80]

For three years Congress resisted this pressure. By 1975, however, amendments to the act were reportedly being pushed by almost everyone: industry, the provider sector, third-party payers, and consumer interest groups, including labor unions.[81]

A series of amendments followed. In 1976, P.L. 94–460 deleted dental benefits for children, reduced open enrollment periods, and excused new HMOs from community rating for the first four years of operation.[82] Thus HMOs followed the same path as did Blue Cross over thirty years earlier; they became competitive by eliminating community services.

In 1978 the act was amended again, this time to provide for expanded federal financial commitments, including (1) $164 million for HMO development over the next three years; (2) an increase in the total level of operating deficit loans to HMOs from $2.5 million to $4.5 million; and (3) a provision allowing federal loans to be used for the construction of ambulatory care facilities.[83] The amendment also reflected industry's wish for a completely new kind of management training program specifically directed toward this new delivery form. Industry believed that slow HMO growth rates were more the result of inappropriately trained personnel than scarce capital.[84]

Hospital administrators, trained in the traditional tenets of maximizing occupancy and extending operations, were not seen as appropriately trained.[85]

This development reflects the increasing division between hospital administrators and physicians, part of a long-term process by which physician control is diminished. It represents the first real contradiction between professional and bureaucratic authority in health care delivery, in the sense that its resolution involves drastic changes in the health care system itself. Parallel authority arrangements are no longer viable. The major goal of the new administrators must now be to control physician practices in the interest of cost-efficiency rather than to use them to maintain full beds.

In addition to the regulations of the HMO Act, early HMO development was threatened by the "certificate of need" process within health systems agencies (HSAs). This issue represented a thorny problem for industry. On the one hand, active participation on health planning boards, particularly HSAs, was an important component of industry's cost containment strategy from its inception. A major function of HSAs was the issuance, or withholding, of certificates of need that would permit greater capital expenditures or construction in the traditional health care sector, which industry wished to avoid. On the other hand, HMOs could not possibly develop or expand if certificate of need laws were applied to them before they were adequately equipped to service their memberships. They would not be able to purchase equipment or build facilities in areas where an HSA had determined that the needs of the populace were already adequately met.

Industry favored HMO exemption from this HSA certification process. At the 1978 annual meeting of the Washington Business Group on Health, Howard Veit, Manager of the Office of HMOs, was asked whether there were attempts being made to "educate" the health systems agencies concerning HMOs. He responded that HEW intended to focus on HSAs because they represented a potential roadblock to HMO development.[86] Of course, HSAs could either aid HMOs, by limiting capital purchases in the traditional sector, or harm them, by applying the same standards to HMOs.

In 1979, P.L. 96–79, the Health Planning and Resources Development Amendment, was enacted, preventing the certificate of need process from blocking HMO growth. The original stated purpose of certificates of need was to prevent duplication of services or of expensive capital equipment within a geographical area. P.L. 96–79 allowed certificates to be issued in areas where there were sufficient facilities if existing facilities were seen as too expensive.[87]

Although many HMO advocates protested that the amendment did not go far enough, that the exemption would not benefit their strategy because it applied only to large plans (those with memberships of fifty thousand or more), the law had the potential to achieve other far-reaching effects. For example, *Modern Healthcare* reported in November 1979 that some hospital officials were predicting that it would contribute to the development of hospital-sponsored HMOs.

The federal government also attempted to stimulate HMO enrollments through other kinds of legislative enactments. Shouldice and Shouldice pointed out in 1978 that five major laws either provided enrollment populations or assisted with the planning, development, and operation of HMOs: (1) the HMO Act and its amendments; (2) the Civilian Health and Medical Programs of the Uniformed Services (P.L. 84–569 and P.L. 89–618), which were given the HMO option in 1973; (3) the Federal Employee Health Benefits Act of 1959 (P.L. 86–283); (4) the Social Security Amendment of 1972 (P.L. 92–603), extending the HMO option, which had been available for certain services since 1965; and (5) Veterans Administration services, covered by P.L. 93–82.

As noted above, the FTC has attempted to facilitate HMO development by preventing private practice physicians from denying hospital privileges to HMO physicians. It has also launched price-fixing charges against hospital groups, which the FTC claims prevent hospitals from bargaining with insurance companies and "other prepaid health insurance plans." In 1980 Ohio filed the first antitrust suit in the nation to accuse hospitals of price fixing. The Ohio attorney general accused the Greater Cleveland Hospital Association and its member hospitals (more than 90 percent of the general hospitals in the Cleveland area) of fixing prices of hospital services. The group was accused of conspiring to restrain competition in the pricing of hospital services because it refused to bargain over hospital rates with insurance companies and other prepaid health insurance plans.[88]

Whether or not such suits are successful, they put great pressure on hospitals to bargain with prepaid groups regardless of what their physicians think or want. Blue Cross had already begun to demand cost accounting and to implement cost-cutting initiatives despite opposition from the hospital associations that had formerly controlled Blue Cross. Now the competitive crunch was pushing hospitals to support HMOs over the opposition of physicians.

Both the HMO Act and FTC anti-trust rulings make it possible for HMOs to advertise services. Effective marketing, however, requires more than the freedom to advertise. The HMO strategy called for the use of demographic information to market HMOs to specific populations in defined geographical areas.

In late 1979, *American Medical News* reported that HEW had targeted three cities, Chicago, Philadelphia, and Washington, for promotional campaigns to increase HMO enrollments among federal employees during the Federal Health Benefits Program "open season."[89] With 9 percent of federal employees enrolled, they were already overrepresented among HMO enrollees nationally, when compared with less than 4 percent among all other employees.[90] The same article reported that HEW had identified about sixty cities as areas of high health care costs where the department planned to promote HMOs aggressively.[91]

An important part of HEW promotional strategy was to involve industry in HMO development. Howard Veit told the 1978 meeting of the Washington Business Group on Health that a former Ford Motor Company executive had been serving as its ambassador to the business community.[92]

Industry also studies population groups in order to determine what are the most likely targets for HMO expansion. Kilgren of Ford Motor Company suggests that employers should pay less attention to open enrollment performance and concentrate on new hires. This group represents the best source of new HMO enrollees because they tend to be young people who are forming new households and are unlikely to have established ties with physicians or hospitals. Kilgren advised companies with significant hiring volume to "elim-

inate any obstacles or bias against HMO selection" in their processing of new hires.[93]

The importance of this population group was borne out by the
fact that at a December 1979 interim meeting of the American
Medical Association delegates adopted a resolution to encourage
insurance company coverage for children in order to make private
insurance more competitive with HMOs.[94] Insurance companies were
losing the elite of the insured population, young employed people,
with their low utilization rates.

There is an interesting dynamic here. Health maintenance strategists have worried that HMOs would lose their competitive edge
because they were required to provide more extensive services than
were indemnity plans. But the fact that they offered these services
enabled HMOs to capture the healthiest group in the country, young
employed people, and thus to keep their premiums low. The traditional insurance industry then experienced pressure to extend its
own services, while HMOs attempt to limit theirs.

HMOs do best when they are located in areas with growing or
rapidly changing populations, particularly of young people, with few
physicians. But their development is not restricted to such areas. In
1980 *American Medical News* carried an account of the processes
through which Blue Cross established an HMO for senior citizens,
called Ultracare, in Santa Barbara, California, a community with a
physician-to-patient population ratio of 1 to 300, about 60 percent
higher than the national average. Santa Barbara is a very affluent
community where senior citizens make up 25 percent of the population.[95]

Although the Blue Cross regional manager said Ultracare was
launched because senior citizens in the area came to them and re-
quested it, only 528 senior citizens enrolled in the program; "we
expected more of a groundswell," the manager said.[96]

Ultracare was established in stages. In 1979 Blue Cross of Southern California contracted with the Santa Barbara Medical Foundation Clinic to provide prepaid care for subscribers enrolled in the
Health Net HMO. This is a Blue Cross-sponsored, federally qualified IPA offered by thirty-three medical groups in Southern California. This program was launched without fanfare and marketed
through employers, with barely a protest from the Santa Barbara

medical community. But an organizational apparatus had been constructed that would serve as a basis for further expansion.

Six months later, Blue Cross announced its sponsorship of Ultracare with a $70,000 advertising campaign. Clinic officials were very
enthusiastic about the plan and claimed that such programs could
avert government regulation; however, local physicians appeared to
be more upset by the immediate competitive threat than the prospect of government interference in the future. They complained that
they were excluded from providing patient care to this population
group and that the clinic negotiated lower hospital rates for the
prepaid groups than for the patients of private practitioners. Most
especially they complained about the massive advertising campaign.
Some physicians were investigating the possibility of suing on the
grounds that the advertisements were unethical.

Physicians increasingly experience HMOs and their promotional
and advertising practices as threats. Professional associations have
formally protested "federal subsidies" and "regulations" that benefit
HMOs.[97] Medical societies have also protested federal promotional
initiatives. In particular they have objected to letters HEW sent to
Medicare beneficiaries advising them to enroll in HMOs.[98]

This is an important source of federal aid to HMO development.
Again, the Twin Cities project provides an example of this process.
In that area, the number of Medicare enrollees jumped 22 percent
between January and March of 1983. Medicare enrollment in HMOs
is now 12 percent of the people eligible for the program. If growth
continued at the current rate, it would have reached 20 percent by
1984. Twin Cities HMOs have focused on Medicare enrollment
because it increases cash flow. "A Medicare enrollee is worth about
four times as much as an HMO member under 65. Medicare pays
about $175 a month per enrollee. By comparison, a typical monthly
payment to HMO membership is $35 to $40 dollars."[99] Of course,
this differential is due to the fact that the elderly use many more
services than typical HMO enrollees, who are young employed
people. However, when Medicare patients are enrolled in HMOs,
"they spend one-third to one-half fewer days in a hospital."[100] The
HMOs are able to cut costs largely because they reduce services to
the elderly. Thus changes in Medicare policy are effected through
administrative controls without the necessity for going through the
political process of changing legislation.

Radical medical sociologists such as J. Warren Salmon have predicted that eventually the U.S. health care system may consist almost entirely of a network of HMOs controlled by big business. The ongoing process appears to be much less sweeping. For health maintenance strategists it is almost irrelevant who owns or administers the HMO. Once it is organized, it can survive only by implementing a massive control program, which simultaneously brings about and constitutes a radical reduction of physician authority in health care delivery.

Relatively high HMO enrollment, in the areas where it exists, brings about an acceptance of the HMO concept as a taken-for-granted reality. The initial conflict between HMOs and traditional medicine blurs and the HMO departure, despite its apparent radicalism, excites no one. California provides us with evidence that HMOs have been socially redefined in this way.

San Francisco veterinarian plans to build 1,500 pet HMOs during the next seven years, throughout the United States. Venture, by Lester Schwab, DVM, the Med-Pet Health Care Plan, has been tested on an experimental basis for the past two years in San Francisco with 300 subscribers. The new plan costs subscribers from $7 a month for one animal to $5 each for three or more animals, plus an enrollment fee of $24. . . . The pet HMO is signing up new members at a rate of 20 to 30 per week, although response from veterinarians has been "less than enthusiastic." Dr. Schwab plans to build 10 more HMOs in the Bay area this year.[101]

SUMMARY

Industry's interest in HMO development is well documented and is directed both at cost containment and at the transformation of traditional health care authority arrangements through competitive pressures.

The federal government has enacted a good deal of legislation that facilitates and supports industry's stated goals in this area. Although the first version of the HMO Act was not in keeping with the competitive spirit of the health maintenance strategy, the amendments that followed as well as other government initiatives have been more congruent with the wishes of industry.

Evidence suggests that where HMOs exist they stimulate changes in physicians' practices and reduce professional authority through processes that function at both the micro and macro levels.

At the micro level the HMO:

1. demands control of the treatment and diagnostic decisions of physicians in order to reduce utilization;
2. redefines these treatment and diagnostic decisions that are based on cost-efficiency as "good medical practice";
3. legitimates these redefinitions of medical practice because they are accepted by physicians as experts;
4. destroys the historical coalition between physicians and administrators that exists in traditional systems;
5. in some cases causes fee-for-service practices to help subsidize the prepaid practices aimed at replacing them.

At the larger level:

1. Industry's support for HMOs led to the development of organizations within medicine itself that are antithetical to traditional practice and undermine it from within. These include the new HMOs themselves, the professionals who staff them, both technical and administrative, and formal organizations such as the American Association of Foundations for Medical Care and the American Association of Professional Service Review Organizations.
2. New organizations that function to further support HMO development have emerged outside the medical system. These include the HEW appointed group and the National Association of Employers on Health Maintenance Organizations, which grew out of the Twin Cities Project.
3. Legislation has been enacted that simultaneously forces organized medicine to cease opposition to the developments that threaten professional authority; establishes such opposition as a manifestation of something other than professional knowledge and expertise, probably greed, power hunger, or the wish to conceal inefficiency; and establishes legal procedures as the proper means of control for clinical practice.
4. Industry also undermines historical coalitions between insurers, hospitals, and physicians, as insurers and hospitals respond to competitive pressures from HMOs by starting their own.

At almost every level industry seeks to undermine the authority of physicians as autonomous, free, professional experts as a necessary condition for both implementing cost controls and restructuring the system. The physician is to become a part of a system that is managerial, scientific, legal in character. Direct clinical knowledge is devalued in the face of computer-based research and controls. These controls entail peer review not only of diagnosis and treatment procedures but also of utilization of medical facilities and of fees.

Industry's interest in these controls is not in the prevention or treatment of disease but in cost reduction. In fact, in many areas, especially those related to industrial hazards, the two criteria-effective treatment and cost reduction—run in opposite directions.

Medical delivery systems facilitated and fostered by industry reduce the authority of physicians and undermine their illusion of being autonomous professionals. Physicians under competitive pressure frequently are compelled to surrender control over delivery systems. The fact that they are well paid in the process undoubtedly sweetens the blow. They resist by using interest group strategies where they can; and when they cannot, they join IPAs, subjecting themselves to more benevolent controls than those of closed-panel HMOs. But even in IPAs, the "system," more than the individual physician, begins to dominate medical treatment.

In all these cases, then, the traditional conception and self-conception of the doctor and autonomous professional are under assault. Like other occupational groups in the contemporary world, physicians will be forced to redefine both themselves and their manifest goals (good medical practice) as a condition of economic survival. Three major questions are obviated by this analysis. First, if we grant that physicians have, in the past, overutilized medical services out of greed, to line their own pockets, how can we expect that in systems such as HMOs they would not withhold necessary services for the same reason? Second, why should we believe administrators intent on eliminating services in order to cut costs would guard the public from this new kind of "physician" abuse? And third, what evidence is there that bureaucratic accountability represents a higher moral order than the professional service ethic?

5

Corporate Roles in Health Care Planning

Planning is at the heart of organizational and administrative rationalization; yet within such closed administrative systems as HMOs, it becomes almost invisible. Instead of planning, the control mechanisms that make goal implementation possible become the focal issues. These mechanisms include methods of prepayment, peer and utilization review, reduction of facilities, and administrative procedures, as discussed above. Although HMOs have required legislative support—such as the dual-choice option, federal loan programs, and legalization of professional advertising—to become established, their internal operations are not closely regulated by the state.

When planning is directed at the parameters of the entire system, however, the planning process is usually carried out explicitly by some government agency and the control mechanisms are defined by government regulations. Just as physicians gained power and created a health care empire through their ability to influence legislation, industry must also use government if it is to be successful in achieving its major planning goal—cost containment. In discussing the fact that industry supports government planning in health care while opposing it everywhere else, Goldbeck adopts a defensive tone, stating that it is quite appropriate for business to use "all available tools" to reduce inefficiency and waste.[1]

The Series reflects great ambivalence, being anti-government, while simultaneously reporting and encouraging government involvement in "planning." Acknowledging that the problems in the health care delivery system are "complex," "interlocking," and "self-perpetuating," the Series notes that some companies have shifted their focus from "limited perspectives," such as controlling benefit packages and rationalizing in-house services, to a "global view" of the health care system as a whole. When the focus shifts to this broader view, the "logical" step for industry is to take an "active consumer role," to effect direct intervention in the planning process. This takes place at two different levels. Corporate executives may expand the traditional roles they have played as hospital trustees, or they may participate directly in federal and state health planning and regulation.[2] In the latter case industry becomes directly involved with government planners.

HOSPITAL TRUSTEESHIPS

The Series depicts the historical role of industry representatives serving as hospital trustees as a philanthropic one, although the political value of philanthropy is fairly obvious. Noting that many trustees on hospital boards have historically been from the private business sector, the Series states that these trustees were motivated by the wish for "prestige" and "self-fulfillment." They gave their loyalty to the institutions on whose boards they sat, not to the broader community or, "less, still to the industries from which they have come."[3]

As the costs of health care rose, the business community began to express concern and corporations began to see in their representation on hospital boards an opportunity to influence decisions that would contain costs. Business executives serving as trustees began to experience conflicts: their corporations were becoming alarmed over rising hospital costs and wanted the boards to exercise some control, but, the Series notes, "the hospital's incentive system still called for relatively unconditional growth and expansion."[4] Instead of working in industry's favor, the philanthropic role, with its emphasis on non-profit institutions and health care, began to conflict with the corporate demand for cost cutting.

Because the cost containment role for executive-trustees was historically new, it became necessary for them to adopt a new point of view, the one espoused by industry. Richard Martin, Manager of Goodyear Tire and Rubber's Health Service Industry Relations in Akron, Ohio, exhorts industry to recognize that in order to get involved it is necessary to adopt a different point of view when dealing with hospitals: "They are not the United Way or Community Chest. They are institutions that are providing a service and are costing your company a lot of money."[5]

In order to eliminate the philanthropic perspective, some kind of educational process was required. Some companies have initiated hospital trustee training programs for their executives, which are available to any members of hospital boards who want to use them. Alcoa is a notable example.[6] Goldbeck reports that these training programs are being developed by several major employers whose officers serve on the boards of HSAs and hospitals and that a national training resource is being developed by the WBGH.[7]

In this process the reality of issues in the health care sector is redefined. Richard Martin of Goodyear describes this new reality with a very clear message. Trustees must learn that physicians do not need what they say they need; they are not making medical decisions but financial ones. The trustees are better equipped to make those decisions in a way that will serve the public interest.[8]

The Series observes that the role of trustees is expanding in two dimensions, in both managing hospitals internally and coordinating them with neighboring facilities. Internal management cannot be left to hospital administrators because a dual-authority arrangement exists within hospitals, which often means that there are no controls or that the medical and administrative staffs balance each other out.[9]

Thus industry recognizes that the interests of physicians and administrators often coincide as the hospital system is presently constituted. Consequently, administrators are unlikely to be agents of change in the desired directions. Trustees must take the responsibility.[10]

At the level of external relations of the hospital, activities by Alcoa executives provide an example of ways in which hospital trustees coordinate neighboring facilities. For years these executives have sat on the hospital boards of communities in which Alcoa's plants were located. In early 1977 a survey by the WBGH revealed that in Alcoa's sixteen plant locations, nineteen Alcoa employees were serving on hospital boards, four as presidents and fifteen as board members.[11] The Series provides an account of the way in which Alcoa executives have "coordinated" health care in their areas. Coordination, the account reveals, includes as a major component the consolidation of hospitals. The manager on one of its West Coast locations attended more than fifty meetings, some as much as one hundred miles away to learn about consolidation processes. That manager then worked with representatives of several other companies to consolidate two community hospitals.[12]

Such consolidations are far more likely to occur if promoted by interests outside the hospitals themselves. Thus Alcoa and other companies, having a dominant interest in cost containment, see the role of the trustee as one of reducing or eliminating facilities, while providers, physicians, and administrators alike have historically attempted to expand them. In attempting to achieve these relatively new corporate goals, business executives have had to give a rather large time commitment to their role as trustees.

The provider press reflects reactions to these new activities by executive trustees. A 1980 cover story in *Modern Healthcare* reported that hospital executives and their boards were making "urgent" plans to increase educational programs for hospital trustees, both to better equip them for complicated hospital planning and to play larger roles as health industry representatives in Washington.[13] Officers of their boards and other trustees are increasingly being sent to seminars, one of the most popular of which is the four-and-one-half-day medical staff and trustee forum put on by the Estes Park Institute, Englewood, Colorado, which was one of six such organizations funded by the Kellogg Foundation in the late 1970's. Trustee education programs are now being planned by the American College of Hospital Administrators, the American Hospital Association, and the Hospital Financial Management Association. Thus the associations of hospitals and their administrators are reacting to increasingly active and critical participation by corporate hospital trustees by setting up their own training programs.

The same issue of *Modern Healthcare* reported that the AMA was taking a stand in favor of physician participation on hospital boards and their action committees: "If such involvement is legally prohibited, local efforts should be initiated to revoke these statutes."[14] This, apparently, is the physicians' defense against non-philanthropic external control.

Such actions by the AMA indicate that administrative support for decisions made by their professional staffs is no longer reflected sufficiently in the decisions of hospital governing bodies as to make direct involvement by physicians unnecessary. The physicians' interests are no longer structurally supported in an unproblematic way; the profession is forced increasingly to function effectively as an interest group.

HEALTH CARE SYSTEM REGULATION

Access to health care has increased radically for large segments of the American population during the last thirty-five years, largely as a product of government policy. This growth resulted in numerous problems within the delivery system. Federal and state governments had enacted a large body of legislation designed specifically to deal with those problems, especially during the last fifteen years. That legislation was often fragmented and uncoordinated and contributed to an even greater expansion of the system.

The major problems of health delivery that legislation was originally designed to address were inadequate facilities and maldistribution of patient access to the system; insufficient professional personnel; and, most recently, problems of overexpansion, wasteful duplication, and utilization control.

Legislation such as the Hospital Survey and Construction Act of 1946 (the Hill-Burton Act) and its subsequent amendments was intended to expand health care facilities. The act provided for federally assisted construction and renovation to deal with the shortage of hospitals in the early post-World War II era, especially in rural areas where hospital facilities were virtually nonexistent. Later amendments extended the program to include funding for hospital utilization research, construction of nursing homes, and construction of outpatient community health facilities.[15]

Besides Hill-Burton, at least seven federal health construction programs were initiated, involving six different federal departments or agencies.[16] These programs often lacked controls and were not coordinated with each other, with the result that different government agencies (HEW and the Small Business Administration, for example) have in some cases made grants or loans to competing hospitals in the same areas, resulting in the kind of waste and overexpansion for which the health care system is so often criticized.[17]

The 1960's in particular was a time of great federal involvement in health care; during President Johnson's administration, "Congress enacted 51 pieces of health legislation, administered through 400 different authorities."[18]

Problems of maldistribution of patient access were addressed through Titles XVIII and XIX of the 1965 Social Security Amendments to the Medicare and Medicaid programs, which were intended to provide financial relief to the indigent and elderly for their medical care. These programs, too, were implemented without controls, as discussed in chapter 2, but the lack ultimately stimulated development of peer review and utilization legislation to fill the gap. One set of legislation was designed to expand access; another, to ration it.

Shortages of professional personnel were addressed by several pieces of legislation, including the Nurse Training Act of 1964 and the Allied Health Professions Personnel Training Act of 1971 (P.L. 92–157). Although the Comprehensive Health Manpower Training Act attempted to coordinate various earlier pieces of legislation, "as many as 14 separate federal departments and agencies are engaged in programs of health training and education."[19]

All the training programs listed above were designed to alleviate problems of personnel shortages and maldistribution through a variety of economic incentives, but the Comprehensive Health Manpower Training Act of 1971 attempted to control costs and set professional standards as well.[20]

Legislation intended to provide a framework to coordinate health care planning has also been enacted. For example, the Regional Medical Program (the Heart Disease, Cancer, and Stroke Amendments, P.L. 89–239) of 1965 attempted to center voluntary regional planning programs around teaching hospitals, as suggested by a 1964 presidential commission headed by Dr. Michael De-Bakey. The AMA lobbied furiously against this legislation and won what Krause calls the "American Medical Association amendment," which stipulated that regional medical programs were not to interfere with existing patterns or methods of financing either patient care or professional practice or with the administration of hospitals.[21] In return, the AMA did not obstruct President Johnson's Medicare program.[22]

A second piece of legislation in this category is the Comprehensive Health Planning and Service Act of 1966 (P.L. 89–749), called Partnership for Health. This act aimed at consolidation of all existing project and formula grants to states.[23] All concerned parties were to be included in a cooperative health planning process, including the federal and state governments, voluntary hospitals, health and welfare councils, and consumers. Consumer majorities on planning boards were mandated. This legislation also contained the American Medical Association amendment, and, Krause maintains, "consumers" were defined "with absolute cynicism," often including "retired physicians, administrators of homes for the aged, and directors of social service departments."[24] Minority consumers, such as blacks, tended to be professionals. A sample taken by the Organization for Social and Technical Innovation found that of fifty-seven consumers, only two were both poor and black or brown.[25] Thus the so-called consumer members were more representative of providers than of health care users.

Sylvia Law maintains that the Comprehensive Health Planning Program was "wholly ineffective" and attributes that failure both to the prohibition against interference with existing patterns of private medical practice, which was the primary cause of overconstruction and unnecessary utilization of hospitals, and to an overreliance by the program on voluntary cooperation of the hospital industry.[26]

Largely as a result of the failure of the planning law, state legislatures began passing certificate of need[27] legislation in the 1970's "to deal with the increasingly obvious and serious problems of overconstruction and to avoid stronger federal intervention."[28] These laws were designed to prohibit large expenditures on health care facilities without a prior determination by a government planning agency that they were necessary. The first such laws were passed in the 1960's in states where overconstruction had already begun to be a problem. The first was enacted in New York State in 1964, followed by Rhode Island (1968), Maryland (1968), Connecticut (1969), and California (1970).[29] By the early 1970's, certificate of need laws were in effect in twenty-six states.[30]

In 1972 Congress enacted the first federal certificate of need legislation, P.L. 92–603, which amended the Social Security Act. It stipulated that the federally funded child health, medicare, and medicaid programs could not be used to support "unnecessary cap-

ital expenditures" by health care facilities or health maintenance organizations. Under this law, funds for interest, depreciation, or div-
idends may be withheld from the expansion or consolidation of
unnecessary facilities. Although participation in the program is voluntary, "currently thirty-seven states have agreements with DHEW
to administer Section 1122."[31]

In sum, these early legislative attempts at overall control or coordination of health services were few and unsuccessful. Over-
whelmingly, the literature reflects an image of proliferating legislation that never accomplished its stated goals or that, in the long
run, resulted in more complex problems. For example, the period
from 1946 to 1967 is described by Stevens as the "period of investment" by the federal government in hospital construction and
renovation, as well as in numerous other programs.[32] That period
ended not with an adequate bed supply but with hospital services
in major cities near the point of "breakdown" and with "one-third
of the nation's hospital beds in 'obsolete condition,' " according to
Stevens, who called for a rationalization "at all governmental and
community levels" of the programs that now exist. She blamed the
current fragmentation on the course public welfare programs have
taken historically. They have been "designed to support state or local efforts, financed through formula and other grants without federal responsibility"; it is essential, she argued, that such responsibility be taken.[33]

Stevens documented the situation as it existed in the mid–1960's.
By 1975, Law reported a "glut" in the numbers of hospital beds.

Various studies put the number of excess empty beds in the United States
in 1975 at between 67,000 and 110,000. Each bed costs $50,000 or more
to construct and equip. It costs, again on the average, about $20,000 a
year to meet the fixed costs of an unoccupied hospital bed.[34]

Alford analyzed the situation from a different perspective than did
Stevens and Law. He did not attribute the failure of health care legislation to a lack of planning and coordination. Noting that the federal government is often seen as a "major force in reforming health
care" because of its extensive enactments, he maintains that its activities have actually "intensified the problems." This is so because
government agencies do not plan and regulate in the public interest

independently of other social forces; rather, they are "likely to become instruments for one or another part of the private sector." The segment of the private sector to which Alford refers here is hospitals.[35]

Alford focuses on the conflict within the health care system itself between "dominant," "challenging," and "repressed" "structural interests."[36] The professional monopoly of physicians is his primary example of a dominant structural interest. Changing factors in the health care system, such as technological developments and expanded and transformed divisions of labor, both of which are associated with shifting rewards to different occupational groups within health care, are creating new structural interests (Alford calls them "corporate rationalizers") that challenge the dominant ones. These challenging interests are also incapable of truly integrating and coordinating health care, however, because the conflict between dominant and challenging interests is "contained within an institutional framework" that prevents the challengers from generating enough "social power."[37] Among these new corporate rationalizers Alford includes hospital administrators, medical schools, government health planners, and the public health agencies and researchers, all components of the health care system, broadly defined. But Alford does not include rationalizing interests external to the system, such as industry.

Industry first began to provide organized support for certain health care regulations in the 1970's. If one considers the history of legislative failures described above, some obvious questions present themselves. Given real political circumstances, could any kind of legislation be effective? Could overall planning legislation get passed unscathed by the demands of lobbyists for the various structural interests? What role does industry play in this process? Could industry substantially alter the structure of the health care system? And, finally, how is traditional, professional authority affected by industry's intervention in the legislative planning process.

RATIONALIZING LAWS—THE HEALTH SYSTEMS AGENCIES

The National Health Planning and Resources Development Act of 1974 (P.L. 93–641) was the culmination of attempts by federal and state governments to introduce broad-range planning into the American health care system. It was designed to reorganize the Comprehensive Health Planning Program, the Hill-Burton program, and the Regional Medical Program. It was the first legislation either to attempt to coordinate the entire health care system through the activities of boards with mandated majorities of consumers or to include a sanctioning mechanism (certificate of need) to prevent unnecessary construction or capital expenditures.

The act established 212 local health systems agencies (HSAs) and, in each state, a statewide health coordinating council and a state health planning and development agency. Consumer majorities were mandated; and "provider" was defined in a more rigorous way than under the 1966 Comprehensive Health Planning Act. Neither hospital trustees nor their wives could be classified as a consumer under this act; instead they were defined as "indirect providers."[38] This reflects the position trustees have traditionally had on their boards, as described above. However, the amendments of 1979 removed trustees from this category and made it possible for them to serve on their local HSAs. This appears to be a result of corporate lobbying activities to facilitate industry's participation in health care planning, an often-stated and vital initiative for both cost containment and reshaping health care delivery. In November 1979, *Modern Healthcare* reported that "corporate executives serving on hospital boards have been reclassified as consumers, making it easier for them to be elected to HSA boards."[39]

Each HSA was charged with producing various kinds of health plans for its area, reviewing and ruling on applications by local providers for federal funds, and issuing (or refusing to issue) certificates of need for capital expenditures by institutions delivering health services. The act did not include expenditures by private physicians.

The certificate of need (CON) program gave planners the power to exercise control in the system for the first time; P.L. 93–641 included a sanctioning mechanism—the withholding of federal funding. States that did not develop and administer CON programs would lose Public Health Service funds. By September 1977, thirty-six states had passed some form of CON legislation. The remaining fourteen were expected to enact legislation soon.[40]

Industry, despite its historic opposition to any kind of government intervention, supported the act and attempted to extend its provisions to cover purchases of capital equipment by private physicians in their offices and for out-of-hospital facilities.[41] Physicians have fought such extensions bitterly for years. For instance, *American Medical News* reported in December 1979 that they were a topic of great concern at the interim meeting of the AMA. For years the AMA had lobbied for modification of P.L. 93–641. But when it was finally done, the new version, P.L. 96–79, was "even more noxious than the original, according to some AMA delegates."[42]

The "noxious" features of which the AMA delegates complained were extensions of CON requirements to private practice and exemption of health maintenance organizations from CON provisions, two of the features most supported by industry and most opposed by the AMA.

Here, again, as in the case of the early legislative mandates for utilization review, these two features, as written, have more symbolic than practical consequences for fee-for-service physicians. It establishes the principle of regulation of private practice and special treatment for HMOs but will not be applicable in many cases. This is so for two reasons. First, CON was extended to cover equipment expenditures greater than $150,000 in physicians' offices, but only if the equipment were to be used for in-patient care. The majority of private offices, where only ambulatory services are delivered, will be unaffected.

Second, only HMOs with memberships in excess of 50,000 are exempted from CON requirements. This will benefit the older, well-established plans, but will not stimulate the development of new ones, which was industry's main objective in supporting this amendment. Thus neither physicians nor industry got exactly what they wanted.

Industry, however, has more reason to rejoice than the AMA. According to Clark Havighurst, the modified health planning law is expected to stimulate competition in the health care sector by allowing expansion of new, free-standing facilities while regulating certain hospital-based services. In addition, the new law requires planners to consider the impact each certificate of need application will have on competitive facilities. This means that if a traditional facility applied for a CON to update aging facilities, it could be denied on the grounds that such improvements might eliminate competition in the area. Havighurst helped write the competitive provisions. He does not, however, advocate the complete elimination of regulation from the health care marketplace. Some must be maintained to protect unprofitable, indigent patients, he argues: "Community hospitals that incur heavy charity care loads and university-based teaching hospitals may have the most difficulty with the amendments. Regulators should protect facilities in extreme cases where indigent care is in jeopardy."[43]

The exemption of physicians' offices from CON regulations stimulated a new conflict of interests between physicians and hospitals. One prominent spokesperson for the hospital industry, John J. Horty, urged hospital associations to lobby for legislation that would apply CON provisions to the clinics, surgicenters, or offices of private physicians. Otherwise, exemption from these provisions may enable physicians to "siphon patients away from hospitals." Horty points out that the law does not distinguish between the traditional doctor's office and that of the modern physician, "which in some instances are expansive clinics with many employees and quite expensive equipment—fully capable of performing many of the functions of hospitals." The planning act, whether intentionally or not, helps maximize the "profits of physicians at the direct expense of hospitals," he charges. Speaking for the hospitals as a separate institution, Horty states that this situation is the result of "pressures from the medical lobby" and urges that hospitals send Congress the "message that hospitals are being discriminated against."[44]

The demands that CONs be extended to physicians' offices have often been made by industry. However, industry also supports the development of alternative treatment centers such as clinics and surgicenters, both of which are under attack by Horty and the hospital associations. Industry urged third-party payers to use reimbursement policies to stimulate their development. Industry appears to have enjoyed a triple victory: it has established the principle that private practice is not above regulation, which infuriates physicians; the alternative forms that industry supports have escaped regulation, at the expense of hospitals; and the process has added to the rift in the historic coalition between hospitals and physicians.

By 1979 the provider press indicated that there was increasing conflict between physicians and administrators in hospitals. P/K Associates, Inc., which prepares a column titled "Phonescan" for *Hospitals* had for several years conducted telephone interviews with random samples of physicians concerning a variety of relevant topics. When "Phonescan" personnel became aware of this increase in conflict, they conducted interviews with fifty physicians and fifty administrators to investigate it.

All respondents agreed that substantial antagonisms exist between the two groups. The majority of physicians thought hospital administrators were "aloof, insecure, autocratic bureaucrats who were too much concerned with finances and too little concerned with patient care," and the majority of administrators thought physicians were "egotistical bumblers who are unable to organize their own lives or records, and who are constantly rebelling against the better organized administrators."[45]

Many physicians stated they thought the problem was not resolvable. One physician said, "There is no reason why the people who run the business—the hospital administrators—and the people who care for the immediate needs of sick people should have anything in common." The "Phonescan" interviewers concluded that the assessments of each group concerning the other were accurate. The antagonisms were a result of the fact that their goals, as they perceived them, were often at cross-purposes. The major sources of conflict, cited equally, were cost containment and general red tape.[46] Both issues emerged largely as the results of the drive for cost-efficiency from every direction and by government regulations, all of which are supported by industry.

The boundary between professional and administrative responsibility appears to have blurred in the minds of the immediate participants in the conflict. For example, the director of a voluntary hospital in Massachusetts said, "The largest problem is that there's no clear idea as to which are the doctors' responsibilities and which the administrators'." Other administrators expressed the belief that "the resulting antagonisms will lead to an impasse within 3 years."[47]

The problem of delineating clear areas of responsibility seems directly related to cost containment goals. Many of the cost-cutting initiatives aimed at by industry were intended to contain costs by directly affecting the way those physicians practice medicine. This fact is often concealed behind shifting definitions of reality. For example, in the past hospitals have ordered the kinds of instruments physicians have said they needed in order to practice "good medicine." Now, with group buying and multi-hospital systems becoming so important in hospital management, administrators would like to standardize purchasing. As one administrator puts it:

A lot of my time is spent telling the doctors here that they don't understand anything about the financial dealings required to run a hospital. One of them likes this kind of instrument and another likes that kind of instrument, and they both want them even though it just isn't cost effective. But when I tell them that, they say I'm interfering with the practice of good medicine.[48]

At the larger level the problem of excess beds provides an example of shifts in definitions of reality. By the mid–1970's, almost all observers, regardless of their political or theoretical orientations, agreed that the United States had too many hospital beds.[49] Part of what was happening was that definitions of what constituted excess beds were being established for the first time.

Sylvia Law defines as the "conservative ideal" an 85 percent occupancy rate of beds within a given hospital. The other 15 percent are assumed to be needed to "accommodate fluctuating patient loads"; anything beyond that constitutes an "excess." But Law includes in her category "excess beds" those which are "occupied by people who do not need to be in the hospital" as well as those which are actually empty.[50]

The idea that patients are hospitalized unnecessarily was first expressed by planners and those involved in peer and utilization review for government, not by the physicians or hospitals treating those patients. Therefore, this perception of excess beds was new and immediately created a new concept: an occupied excess bed. The problem was that this concept was entirely undocumented. No data had been collected or could have existed according to which any planner could say what constituted the actual number of truly necessary beds in a given area.

Planners only had bed-population ratios drawn from atypical populations, such as young families with employed, unionized, male household heads, who belonged to established HMOs such as the Kaiser Foundation. As noted above, it had always been the policy of such groups to maintain a tight bed supply for their relatively healthy populations.[51]

When HEW issued guidelines for health systems agencies to evaluate certificates of need in January 1978, they stipulated a maximum of 4.0 hospital beds per 1,000 persons in a health service area,[52] compared with the national average of 6.5 beds for 1,000 persons.[53] The HEW regulation stipulated about the same ratio as the Kaiser plan. Of the 213 health systems agency service areas studied during 1978, only 14 met the HEW guidelines.[54] Since virtually no areas met the guidelines, it seems reasonable to assume that they were based on the experiences of prepaid group plan membership, not those of the larger, more typical population.

In some states planners have reacted very aggressively to reduce facilities in keeping with the HEW guidelines. Michigan began plans immediately to shut down more than five thousand of its forty thousand beds. In California a special committee appointed by Governor Jerry Brown recommended that "unneeded and inappropriate hospitals" be shut down "and that the State Health Facilities Commission be changed to a Public Utilities Commission structure" designed to control hospital budgets and rates. The committee also recommended that a pilot project be carried out "in which hospitals in San Francisco, San Diego, and San Bernardino counties would be forced either to negotiate rates with insurance companies or to collect from patients directly." Governor Brown charged that hospitals "have a license to steal" and called his committee recommendations "a national model for health care."[55]

Some states took planning controls even further than the federal planners. For example, by 1979 state health planners in Rhode Island and Hawaii hoped to use certificates of need to control the numbers of physicians practicing in their states: "A state agency would decide the number of MDs needed, and licenses to practice would be denied once the quotas had been filled." New York and California also wanted to control the numbers of physicians in their states by limiting the number or size of residency programs. In California

residency programs would be allocated among teaching hospitals by the Office of Statewide Health Planning and Development, and certified by the Board of Medical Quality Assurance according to the state's need for program graduates as determined by the planning agency. Residents enrolled in uncertified training programs could be denied licenses to practice."[56]

These developments represented a complete reversal of earlier positions taken by planners and professional associations. During the fifteen years before 1979, training programs for both physician and paraprofessionals had been encouraged by planners, who believed that increasing the numbers of physicians and other direct providers would increase competition and bring market mechanisms into play. This would both reduce physicians' fees and health care costs. At first the AMA opposed these training programs. But when, contrary to the planners' predictions, both fees and utilization rates began to rise, it began to support them actively. It is utilization, not physicians' fees, that is the significant factor in health care cost containment. Research findings at that time indicated that utilization increased directly with the numbers of physicians in practice. Because each physician ordered services costing hundreds of thousands of dollars a year, reducing their numbers became the new formula to reduce utilization rates and costs.[57] Thus the AMA and planners traded positions. The AMA opposed efforts to cut back on the training programs that it initially opposed, while planners looked for ways to practice professional birth control.

Despite the extensiveness of the planning act of 1974, the bitter opposition it had received from providers, its sanctioning provisions, and its mandated consumer majorities serving on HSA boards, some medical sociologists were pessimistic about its capacity to achieve its goals. Krause stated that the act "hands even more power to the regulated."[58] Law complained that even though it provided for reviews every five years to certify continuing need for established facilities and services, the act contains no enforcement mechanisms if beds are found to be unnecessary.[59] This view contrasts sharply with the more optimistic image in the Series of the potential power of HSAs to restructure the health care system.

The explanation for this discrepancy may be based in part on different bases for the analyses of the planning process. Medical sociologists often focus on the political nature and functions of planning. They may conclude, as did Alford, that existing "structural interests" are able either to prevent the implementation of plans or to co-opt the plans to suit their own interests.[60] Others, like Krause, may focus on the manifest content of the plans themselves and conclude they are mere "ideological statements";[61] Alford and Krause, in effect, then agree. Citing a study of Frieden and Peters of thirty-three health plans, Krause criticizes them on the grounds that they are "verbal statements made about health services systems that describe no specific ends, no alternatives, with only vague goals, with little consideration of physical or ecological variables, and almost no relevant data analysis, and no target date for implementation."[62] Krause concludes that planning can be seen as a simple political activity in the direct sense of the term.

Krause, Alford, Stevens, and others see this political process as working in the interest of the regulated, the providers, an assessment often made of the regulatory process in general. This view, as a general thesis, does not deal with the specific phenomenon in question: namely, that regulation functions in the interest of the regulated largely because the regulation is supported by other, powerful elements that impinge upon the institutional network. This is an extension of Alford's "structural interest" theory; he takes as his "structure" the health care system as an internal whole, though he defines it to include government agencies. A broader concept of "structure" would include institutions and agencies of the larger social environment, including perhaps the most powerful social institutions in contemporary history, the modern corporation.

The theorists of industry themselves take this more extended perspective. Although the Series takes full account of the ways in which professionals and their organizations exercise political pressure to influence legislation in their own interest, it does not accept the idea that professional opposition can permanently obstruct change in the health care system. Conference Board publications and the Series both assume that government regulations will always be determined by external factors, that is, various mixes of interest group pressures. The history of peer standards review organizations provides good evidence for this view. Both the Series and medical sociologists are aware of the ways in which providers have been able to control peer review as the price for allowing it to exist at all. However, industry, we have found, succeeded in reversing that control to some extent and using the PSROs in their own interest.

In the case of health planning, industry takes the position that professional opposition can be balanced and ultimately overwhelmed by business support for selected government planning. This does not mean that industry supports the goals that government in the past has traditionally tried to implement. Industry supports only government cost containment goals. When government has increased costs by expanding access and facilities, industry has not been so sanguine. Only under the cost containment and restrictive policies of recent years has industry supported government regulation.

INDUSTRY AND HEALTH SYSTEMS AGENCIES

Industry's major motive for acting in the health care sector is to contain costs. Toward that end, its actions in the health systems agency system are directed toward the long-term goal of restructuring health care delivery. As Richard Martin of Goodyear says, "Health planning is not going to save big money today, or even tomorrow, but it is a rational start to get some sense of efficiency into the system."[63]

Industry sees the National Health Planning and Resources Development Act of 1974 (P.L. 93–641) primarily as a means of rationalizing the system, not as an immediate way to provide low-cost health care. Goldbeck makes this distinction clear. For him the major purpose of the act is to ration limited resources for which there is an "insatiable demand." Goldbeck evaluates and contrasts the act with its "ineffective predecessors." The certificate of need provision is the first most important distinction because, in effect, it transforms the planner into the regulator. Effective planning requires sanctioning power, which is provided by the CON process, to insure that decisions made by consumers may be implemented over the opposition of the providers who do not wish to relinquish authority. In the future, Goldbeck predicts, more control will be exercised. Periodically, existing facilities will have to be recertified. Those that no longer serve their intended purpose will be decertified.[64]

A second major difference between the P.L. 93–641 era and the past, Goldbeck points out, is that consumers, not providers, have majority control of HSAs; and consumers are defined in such a way as to include the "major purchasers of medical care." The major purchaser is, of course, industry, not the patient in Goldbeck's view.

A third feature that is new to P.L. 93–641 is that it recognizes that provider expertise is not essential to a policy-making role.

Goldbeck states that neither the physician nor the hospital administrator will set priorities for community health.[65] Industry, the purchaser, will provide its own, bureaucratic expertise.

Goldbeck points out that in order to be effective consumers must be well informed and have time to devote to HSA activities. This sets the scene for education programs launched by industry, whose employees often devote considerable time to this activity, presumably because it is in the interest of the company. Business executives thus meet these qualifications. The professional and administrative expertise of physicians and hospital administrators are lumped together and then pronounced unnecessary; they will no longer be dominant in the policy-making process.

For all these reasons, Goldbeck sees HSAs as excellent vehicles to be used by industry for the purpose of reshaping local medical care delivery.

Goldbeck points out that support for federal planning regulations puts industry into positions that are antithetical with those it has taken historically on other issues. For example, where health care issues are concerned, industry encourages not competition but cooperation: companies and unions are encouraged to "share data" and combine their economic and political clout. Individual hospitals are praised for sharing services and facilities: for example, he cites a 1977 report from the American Hospital Association stating that the cooperative efforts of a relatively few hospitals had saved millions of dollars. The financial community is encouraged to cooperate with health planners. When approached to make loans for capital equipment or construction, lenders should be "responsible." They should ascertain whether the proposed facility is really needed. If it is not, they should cooperate with the HSA and refuse to make the loan in spite of the fact that profits can be made whether the facility is needed or not. This potential for profit by business is, of course, a major reason that planning is needed in the first place, although Goldbeck does not linger on this point. Without such cooperation from financial agents, Goldbeck argues, physicians will circumvent the planning process by purchasing large, expensive and unnecessary capital equipment for their private offices.[66]

The Series notes that in all these cases existing anti-trust policies are in conflict with health care cost containment policies.[67] Industry has "traditionally and philosophically" supported government intervention "at the lowest possible level of political jurisdiction," making individual states more acceptable than the federal government for health policy administration. (In this case, industry's position is reversed. This may be because it is only in this case that it wishes regulation to be effective.) Goldbeck laments the fact that the states have shown themselves to be even less competent than the federal government in administering health programs. State legislative efforts conflict with each other and with federal regulations, and this costs employers who operate across state lines additional money.[68]

The Series notes with approval the fact that the latest health planning efforts have been more effective than earlier ones. However, it points out two weaknesses in the HSAs. First, although they have more authority than did their predecessors, they are still unable to control third-party financing decisions effectively. These decisions determine to a large extent how health services will be organized and delivered.[69]

The extent to which regulatory agencies can control third-party funding is contingent on the kind of power bases the agencies can build. If the consumers who sit on HSA boards represent corporations who negotiate large employee health insurance contracts, the power of the HSA can be very great. Thus government HSA regulation largely increases industry's control in planning as it has in other areas, such as peer review.

Second, the Series states that full funding of the HSAs has been delayed and, in any event, will probably be inadequate to attract and hold a staff with as much technical expertise as that of the providers they will be trying to regulate.[70] Thus the legitimating power of technical expertise remains a thorn in the side of the merely efficient bureaucrat.

Industry can help solve these problems, the Series states. First, it can use its political and economic power, as a payer for health care, to help the HSA expand its power base and increase its strength. Second, industry can lend staff to the HSA and provide direct technical assistance. In this case, corporate personnel would, to some extent, control the health systems agency.

Third, industry can and does provide direct financial support to HSAs. As Richard Martin of Goodyear, President of the Akron-area HSA, points out, this is necessary because the funds allocated by the federal government are completely inadequate. In Akron, Martin's group went to the corporate community and made the case that budgeting $125 million, nationally, to plan for a $140 billion expenditure was to beg failure. Martin reports that the Akron HSA was able to add staff in spite of reductions in federal support in 1976 because of corporate contributions.[71]

Fourth, industry can provide "leadership." In fact, this is an old role for the business sector, as Anthony Mott, Executive Director of the Finger Lakes HSA of Rochester, New York, points out. Mott asserts that in a number of cities, including Rochester, Pittsburgh, Cleveland, and Detroit, health planning has been around on a voluntary basis for twenty or thirty years. Although the reasons for planning varied from city to city, in Rochester it was clearly the result of intervention by industry.[72]

The Series uses the Rochester experience to exemplify what can be achieved through a close interaction between private corporations, financial institutions, and a government agency. A senior executive at Eastman Kodak, Marion Folsome, was able to persuade the city's banks "to stop the flow of money into recalcitrant health care institutions." As a result, health planners have been able to keep down hospital construction while emphasizing the development of alternative facilities such as out-patient clinics and neighborhood health centers. Folsome left Eastman Kodak to become secretary of HEW. The late Joe Wilson of Xerox then became "Rochester's corporate Health Czar."[73]

The Series cites other, similar examples of industry participation in the health planning process.[74] Thus in Detroit, General Motors combined with Ford and Chrysler to develop a very comprehensive cost containment plan. These companies worked very closely with community health planners. Industry involvement in community health planning has become a tradition in Pittsburgh, Pennsylvania; Portland, Maine; and Wausau, Wisconsin.[75]

Those who have been successful in these activities have very positive evaluations. Martin of Goodyear states that with the aid of company resources, almost anything can be achieved through HSAs.[76]

Despite the reported successes, Mott says that in some regions where businesses and industries have attempted to participate in the HSAs, they have unaccountably been firmly rejected.[77] It is a reasonable assumption that in these cases the HSAs were dominated by providers. Thus, John Brown of Genesco reports that it took a lot of time and effort to get on the board in his area because providers controlled the entire HSA, including the projects review and executive committees.[78]

Philip R. Davis, Executive Director of the Chicago HSA, suggests another possible reason—conflicting views of the proper functions of the HSA. Davis expressed disapproval of moves by the federal government to back up appropriateness reviews with reimbursement policies; this is exactly the kind of sanctioning mechanism that industry wants. Davis told *Modern Healthcare* that he thought HSAs should act as "facilitators," not as "dictators," and should function as a part of local government, not as private nonprofit corporations: "Private organizations . . . should not be performing government function."[79] This is, of course, exactly the function that industry wishes the HSAs to perform—they should be publicly funded, formally established bodies that have legal sanctioning powers and are under the control of industry. Thus industry wants for itself the control physicians have historically enjoyed.

Joseph Kozlowski of TRW describes some of the ways in which industry approaches and establishes ties with local HSAs.[80] He does so by analyzing the relationship between an effective community planning coalition, the Greater Cleveland Coalition on Health Care Cost Effectiveness, and the local HSA.

Kozlowski and others from the business community participated in a cost containment seminar sponsored by the Case Western Reserve University School of Management, along with other "concerned constituencies," including representatives from business, labor, hospitals, physicians' groups, and others. After the seminars were over, a group of the business participants went around the community trying to find others who were interested in forming a coalition. This took about a year to get organized. The finished product was a board of directors that included representatives for all the "major constituencies" within the community. The board consisted of fifteen members, including two people from the insurance industry (one from the Blues and one representing commercial carriers); two people from business; two from labor; five providers (one from the hospital association, one from the medical society, one dentist, two representing the physician community at large); and a "catch-all category" of four people, including academics, consumers, and others.

Although patients are invisible in this summary and there appears to be a preponderance of provider representatives, Kozlowski reports that no one category dominated the board. Insurance carriers tended to be the "swing votes."

Once the group was established, it opted to find an umbrella organization, rather than setting up a corporation. The best offer came from the local HSA, which provided stenographic help, office supplies, telephone answering services, and a mailing address, without asking anything in return.

This arrangement apparently gave the group maximum freedom. An alternative to it could have been to use the chamber of commerce as the umbrella organization. When asked why the group did not do so, Kozlowski replied that the chamber's bureaucratic structure interfered with the group's flexibility.

It is a fascinating assessment that the chamber of commerce is seen as a more bureaucratically demanding organization than organizations mandated by a federal regulatory act and overseen by the Department of Health, Education, and Welfare (now Health and Human Services).[81]

Commenting on Kozlowski's position, Ronald Hurst, Manager of Health Care Planning at Caterpillar Tractor, member of the Central Illinois Health Systems Agency, and chair of the Peoria Chamber of Commerce's Health Services Committee, observed that the chamber has itself performed the same functions as the Cleveland coalition in Peoria, making it unnecessary to form yet another organization.[82]

Once the organizational phase of the Cleveland coalition was completed, the group delineated five areas in which to establish task forces. These included health education; data base development; provider and hospital efficiency; incentives to ensure cost effectiveness; and processes to rationalize utilization. The only issue having to do with health is the one called health education. All the others have to do with cost and utilization control. Presumably, health education in this context is, like that discussed in chapter 2, designed to alter consumer behavior to make it more cost-efficient.

Kozlowski gives the following piece of advice to other groups interested in following the same pattern: "Don't let yourselves be coopted by anyone. Make sure that you remain business-oriented and don't get pulled into long, academic studies."[83] This is compatible with observations reported above, that health care data are not necessary to make policy designed to cut costs. Thus business co-opts others, but resists the process itself: it is the unco-optable co-optator.

SUMMARY

Industry has attempted to incorporate its initiatives into the health care system by participation in the planning process, both at the micro and macro levels.

At the micro level, it has encouraged and in some cases trained executives serving on hospital boards to take a more active leadership role on the boards and to be more critical of the requests of providers.

At the broader level, industry has supported and participated in regulatory planning by government agencies, including the National Health Planning Act of 1974 and many of its subsequent amendments. This act mandated the creation of a network of regional health systems agencies and the establishment of a certificate of need program to function as a control mechanism. Industry has supported this process and has utilized external means to make them effective. These means include providing funds and personnel to the health systems agencies, encouraging executives to serve on the agencies, influencing lending agencies to deny capital to providers who do not have certificates of need, and manipulating reimbursement policies to deny payments for services provided by facilities or equipment that were constructed or purchased without certificates of need.

These are processes in which the powers of corporate executives and the state are combined to create and support new structures within the health care sector. These structures are staffed by bureaucratic administrators and planners, whose power requires that the authority of traditional providers, both physicians and administrators, be diminished.

These activities are undertaken from one central value base, cost control and containment. And since this is the operative impulse, the organizational drive to cooperation with government, with HSAs, and with others in the professional community is limited. Cooperation, the broadening of access to health care, and the improvement of medical services all appear to be limited by this goal.

6

Provider Adaptations to Structural Pressures

Providers and hospitals have reacted to pressures from industry and government in a variety of ways. The most conscious and planned response has been cooperation between physicians and hospital administrators to forestall further regulation by attempting to cut health care costs themselves. This attempt, the Voluntary Effort, as it is called, often utilizes the same kinds of initiatives advocated by industry in order to promote cost-efficiency.

A second kind of response has been the emergence of a new organizational form in the health delivery system, an administrator-dominated, monolithic, multi-institutional management system. Once in place, these multi-unit systems have a profound effect on the rest of the health care sector. Most importantly from the standpoint of this analysis, they are inherently incompatible with physician-dominated, traditional health care structures.

THE VOLUNTARY EFFORT

Health care providers have responded to political and economic pressures from government and corporate consumers by launching the Voluntary Effort (VE) to contain health care costs. The VE is a coalition that originally included the American Hospital Association, the American Medical Association, and the Federation of American Hospitals, which represents investor-owned, proprietary hospitals. Later the coalition was broadened to include the Blue Cross and Blue Shield Associations, the Health Industry Manufacturers' Association, the Health Insurance Association of America, the National Association of Counties, Virginia Knauer and Associates (consumer consultants), and representatives of business and labor.[1] Participation by labor has been extremely limited.

In December 1977 the VE formed a national steering committee to set policy guidelines and goals for the industry as a whole. The steering committee worked out a fifteen-point program aimed at achieving a significant reduction in the rate of increase in hospital and health care costs. Major goals included a 2 percent reduction in hospital cost increases for both 1978 and 1979; no net increases in hospital beds in 1978; and capital spending in 1978 limited to no more than 80 percent of the last three years' average.

Other points in the program addressed problems in the utilization and productivity of physicians, the role played by third-party payers, the effect of health care insurance as a fringe benefit, the role of government, and ways in which regulations could be made cost-effective.[2]

The VE represents a struggle by health care providers to maintain control over the health care system. Although VE leadership states officially that it cannot succeed without support from the wider community, it is clearly a provider-controlled effort.

In order to maintain control, providers have structured their programs in such a way as to eliminate some of the criticisms directed at them by government, industry, and consumer groups. Thus they have already lost control, to the extent that these "outside groups" have forced them to address issues that they previously had neglected. The question is, Are these serious attempts by providers to make real changes or merely means of avoiding worse alternatives? Such questions can never be resolved by a statement of the programs' intentions. We can only assess effects by looking at the history of the Voluntary Effort and at the extent to which it has or has not implemented effective programs.

Government and the VE

The immediate impetus for the VE was the prospect of federal cost control legislation. Throughout the summer of 1977 the House

Ways and Means Subcommittee on Health worked on a bill to control rapidly rising costs in the health care sector. This topic was being publicly discussed by so many concerned groups, business, consumers, labor, and government, that passage of some kind of federal control system seemed inevitable. According to House member John J. Salmon, in late 1977 Congressman Rostenkowski, Chairman of the subcommittee, was approached by representatives from the health delivery system. They said they wanted to solve the problem themselves and to keep government off their backs. Rostenkowski responded that the subcommittee would also like providers to solve the problem "so we wouldn't have to put government on your back." According to Salmon, the private sector blew the statement up into a "challenge" from government.[3] Salmon expressed surprise that the industry came out in December with specific goals that HEW actuaries found would save as much as the administration's proposal. Congressman Rostenkowski proposed a back-up cost containment program that would go into effect only if the VE failed to achieve its rate reduction increase of 2 percent per year. But the health care industry fought this compromise bill even harder than the original one because, as one provider spokesman told Salmon informally, there was a chance it might actually pass.

Joseph N. Onek, Associate Director, Domestic Policy Staff of the White House, took this opposition as evidence that the proponents of the VE did not, themselves, believe their efforts could succeed and were attempting only to avoid regulation.[4] The cost control bill was defeated in the House in November 1979, after massive lobbying by the health care industry.

Business and the VE

If the VE is to succeed, it is essential that the corporate sector support it; that would mean accepting reform rather than the restructuring of the system. Goldbeck was aware of the strategic value of business support for the VE. He voiced his determination not to be "co-opted" by it and urged industry to make the coalition "accountable": "No statistic that the VE puts out should be accepted by you just because they put it out. . . . The VE can be a cartel, as it has been described, or it can be made accountable. Industry can make the difference."[5]

Conversely, the VE leadership has actively courted business participation. In early 1979 AMA representatives approached executives of U.S. Steel to express concern over the rising cost of health care. The physicians concluded that they shared a commonality of interest with the corporation: "when we discussed this, we learned that we were equally concerned about turning over anything to the government to run. We were equally afraid the government would foul that up, too."[6]

In September 1979, representatives from several leading U.S. corporations were invited to AMA headquarters in Chicago to work out the next stage of the AMA's plan to win business support for its cost control efforts. The AMA leadership intended to have an "education and informational" meeting, but corporate leaders insisted on an "action-oriented program." The meeting was attended by people with authority to launch such programs. Corporate representatives included Jack Shelton, Manager of Employee Insurance Department, Ford Motor Company; George A. Hensarling, Director of Employee Benefits for U.S. Steel; Norbert J. Roberts, M.D., Medical Director for Exxon Corporation; Laurence B. Huston, Jr., Assistant Vice President for Aetna Life and Casualty; and Christopher York, Vice President of Citicorp. They were addressed by James H. Sammons, M.D., Executive Vice President of the AMA. One outcome of this meeting was that the AMA agreed to send some of its top officials to visit seventy-five leading corporations to ask for their views on "the nature of health care problems."[7]

The attempted alliance between the AMA and business is reflected in concrete action at the local level. For example, in January 1980 a meeting was scheduled between Birmingham, Alabama, physicians and businessmen to discuss health care problems in the community. The meeting was a result of a cooperative effort between the American Medical Association and representatives from leading U.S. corporations.[8]

Providers appear to perceive business as actually supportive of the VE, although this interpretation is highly questionable. As observed by Nila Vehar of the Koopers Company, the Voluntary Effort does not appear to have much support from industry: "Mr. Goldbeck . . . does not seem very optimistic about [its] success."[9] It is true that some corporate groups opposed the House cost containment bill and threw their weight against it. Apparently, when the bill failed, providers perceived corporate anti-regulatory interests as identical with their own. This is an inaccurate perception. Corporate leaders are not opposed to regulations that control provider monopolies, only those that interfere with their manipulation of market mechanisms. When corporate leaders speak of keeping the health care system in the private sector, which they often do, they mean in the corporate sector. They expressly do not want it left in the hands of providers. This perspective is stated explicitly throughout the Springer Series, somewhat diffidently at first (by Goldbeck in volume 2), then more strongly by Havighurst later on (in volume 7).

Goldbeck, using a conciliatory tone, stated that industry did not want to alter its comfortable relationship with the provider professions either by shifting to an adversarial posture or by providing direct care; it will do so only if organized medicine fails to change with the needs of health care consumers.[10]

Havighurst sounds a far more strident note, stating that those who consume health care services and pay for insurance will have to depend primarily on "private financing mechanisms, [they] cannot depend on provider cartels such as the VE."[11] Havighurst advocates the use of anti-trust laws to prevent provider groups either from interfering directly with private attempts at innovation or from organizing "half-way measures" for no other purpose than to impede the development of alternative financing and delivery arrangements.[12] Clearly he does not support and is even hostile to the Voluntary Effort.

Insurance Industry and the VE

Insurance companies are often accused of failing to contain health care costs, either because they are thought to be provider controlled or because they do not have economic incentives to do rigorous claim investigation. It is probably an indicator of the success of external attacks on traditional medical practice that insurance companies do not give wholehearted support to the VE. In his keynote address at the March 27, 1979, meeting of the New England Hospital Assembly, Robert Froehlke, President of the Health Insurance Association of America, said "it would be a mistake for the insurance industry to put all its eggs in the VE basket."[13] Froehlke thinks that it is not possible to introduce enough competition into the hospital system to keep costs down and that, therefore, there is a need for some kind of regulation of hospitals.[14]

Kenneth W. White of the Health Insurance Institute also expresses support for "appropriate legislation," including hospital budget review commissions in each state, effective certificate of need programs, and stronger health planning programs.[15]

Again, these views emphasize the desirability of both competition and selected forms of regulation in the health care industry and are expressed throughout the Series by representatives of corporate groups.

Labor and the VE

Paul Earle, Executive Director of the VE, reports that although providers have invited representatives of the AFL-CIO and the UAW to participate in the VE at the national level, they have received negative replies. In fact, the AFL-CIO has formally opposed the VE and has recommended that their affiliates not participate. Bert Seidman of the AFL-CIO states that labor has taken this position because the major tactic for maintaining costs at the level of the voluntary guidelines was to keep wage increases for unorganized hospital workers at 5 percent.[16]

In this case, at least, initiatives taken by the VE do include increasing the efficiency of productivity not of high-paid professional personnel, however, but of one of the lowest-paid groups of workers in this country, the unorganized hospital workers.

Providers and the VE

It is not clear whether the American Hospital Association and the American Medical Association have the support of their members in the VE. Some hospital administrators express resentment that the VE presents them in a bad light, implying that soaring costs are the result of negligence on the part of hospitals. They are also pessimistic about the chances of the VE cost control effort's being successful, given the overall inflation rate. They believe the federal government "manipulated the hospital industry into the Voluntary Effort knowing it would fail."[17]

This perception may be based upon statements made by government spokespeople. For example, Joseph Onek, a representative from the White House, says, "We do not think that, left to itself, the VE will succeed." Onek believes that the current reimbursement system creates disincentives for such an effort.[18] Onek thus expresses the opinion of industry that costs cannot be brought under control without changing the incentives built into the existing third-party reimbursement system.

John Salmon, member of the U.S. House of Representatives, states that Congressman Rostenkowski, Chairman of the House Ways and Means Subcommittee on Health, believes firmly that providers will not exercise voluntary restraint "without some appropriate stimulus."[19]

State hospital associations have been slow to support the VE because of fears that they might be sued under anti-trust legislation. For example, the Hospital Association of Pennsylvania shelved a plan to monitor hospital suppliers and publish a list of those that increased their prices because of fear of a lawsuit.[20]

It is uncertain whether the general membership of the AMA supports the VE. In late 1978 AMA president Tom Nesbitt called for a 1 percent reduction in physicians' fees to bring increases down to or below the overall Consumer Price Index. The AMA's House of Delegates formally endorsed the request in December.[21] Leaders of the AMA, however, were not sure members would comply. The AMA was trying to "raise the consciousness" of physicians, and make them more aware of the costs of tests and services they provide patients, according to Bill Cohan, Director of the AMA's Division of Medical Practice.[22] This is necessary because cost control by physicians involves both physicians' fees and the charges for the treatment and diagnostic procedures they prescribe for their patients. Cohan has primary responsibility for coordinating the AMA's activities in support of the VE. His charge is to survey physicians to determine if they are complying with Nesbitt's request for fee reductions.

The AMA has also worked closely with state medical societies to set up statewide VE committees. In some localities, local medical societies became quite aggressive in their attempts at cost containment. For example, in Texas one county medical society began to report in each issue of its newsletter one fee abuse case that was handled by the group's adjudication committee, "a long-established standing committee of the medical society that reviews all fee complaints from the public as well as from insurance companies." The facts and outcomes of the cases were to be reported but not the names of physicians or patients because of fear of libel suits. However, the spokesperson for the society said, "If this approach doesn't produce some evidence of success, I'd seriously consider [publishing the physicians' names] in the newsletter."[23]

The AMA officially supported these attempts of constituent societies to control fee abuse. In July 1979 the AMA announced that it would "seek legislation to allow constituent medical societies to review reasonableness of MD's charges in order to protect the public." The same month, the AMA House of Delegates passed a resolution "urging the AMA to seek legislation, if needed, to protect medical societies who discipline members who charge excessive fees or exploit their patients.[24] Thus the AMA seems to have developed some sensitivity to the criticism from industry and elsewhere that it functions only as political lobbying apparatus and is not concerned with professional standards of quality or ethics.

Although discussion of physicians' fees are often emotional, the combined charges for the tests and services that physicians order for their patients have far more impact on the total cost of health care than do the fees. In the past it has been an article of faith among physicians that such costs should not determine choices physicians make about patient care. Consequently, physicians have never learned what those costs are. For example, in a Washington, D.C., suburban area a "quiz" on hospital costs revealed that six out of ten physicians "flunked the test on medical charges." As a result, the president of the local medical society, Dr. Leon Block, began sending brochures listing these charges to doctors practicing in the county. Block justified his action by stating that in the past doctors had not taken these costs into account because "their attitude has been to do the right thing with no thought of the cost." There is now pressure on the physicians to change this attitude. Dr. Roger Snyder, Chairman of the Cost Containment Committee of Dr. Block's medical society, said, "while every test has some potential benefit, physicians have to measure in better fashion than they have in the past whether benefits are greater than costs."[25]

Some hospitals began to conduct "cost awareness rounds" as part of regular continuing medical education programs. Darrell Cannon, M.D., spearheaded such rounds at several hospitals in California. Cannon says that "most physicians don't have the vaguest notion of what things they order cost or how the charges for these things are developed, and that's well documented." Cannon got the idea for economic rounds at an AMA Leadership Conference.[26]

Costs are also being introduced into the curricula of medical schools and graduate medical training programs. Many of these programs start early, at the undergraduate level, before the students' clinical habits have been "set."[27]

Whether individual AMA members support the VE policies or not, it is clear that medical societies have attempted to exercise professional control to an unprecedented degree: they are doing so, however, in response to increasing pressure from the external agencies.

There have been differences of opinion between various hospital associations concerning the VE. John J. Horty, President of the National Council of Community Hospitals, has been skeptical of the VE, even though it is supported by both the American Hospital Association and the Federation of American Hospitals.[28]

Horty feels that the American Hospital Association has been effective in its cost containment fight only because of the threat of mandatory controls and that the VE will eventually wear thin. *Modern Healthcare* notes that Horty is implying that the effectiveness of the Voluntary Effort on hospitals and Congress will then weaken. Many health care administrators and economists believe this is already happening. Horty helped found the National Council of Community Hospitals in order to provide an alternative to such mechanisms as the VE: "We began to look at basic ways to restructure the system rather than to be essentially negative or to adopt the government system."[29]

But Horty has occasionally suffered criticism from the rest of the hospital industry when he has supported government policies that other groups oppose.

Mr. Horty attracted the wrath of other hospital industry lobbyists when, flanked by White House and HEW officials, he announced that NCCH supports the administration's "voluntary" goal of a 9.7% limit on increases in hospital expenditure for 1979. The American Hospital Association charged in a wire to state hospital association executives that the NCCH was undercutting the industry's fight against controls. Some colleagues asked NCCH administrators and trustees how they could support the fledgling group.[30]

Horty is not, however, a maverick or pariah in any sense but is a well-respected, often-read and -quoted, and very active participant in activities involving the hospital industry. His controversial position indicates a genuine and deep division in the thinking of leaders of hospital associations on the appropriate role of government regulation and on the desirability of the VE. This division may be a symptom of the changes that have begun to occur in the entire health care system.

PROGNOSIS FOR THE VE

Providers do not appear to have the kind of broad-based support they say they need for the VE to succeed. Government, business, insurance companies, and labor leaders have withheld unconditional support, and some have expressed the view that voluntary cost containment cannot succeed in the long run.

Paul Ellwood, President of InterStudy, a medical and social policy research firm commissioned by the U.S. Chamber of Commerce (among other groups) to study health care costs, both expresses and helps form the opinions of business and community leaders. Ellwood maintains the VE cannot work unless it restructures the incentives of the medical/hospital system. In his judgment, the health care industry is only behaving as it has been rewarded for doing.[31]

The goal of providers is to reform the system from within; government and industry are intent on restructuring it from without. Industry support for the VE is contingent on collaboration by physicians and hospitals with their efforts to change the entire system. These will include drastic reductions in professional authority and autonomy. The VE would, from this perspective, have to become a means for changing the system. By the early 1980's, it seemed more likely that industry would co-opt the VE than the other way around, if for no other reason than the fact that the AMA did not appear to be aware of this possibility.

HEALTH CARE ORGANIZATION AND MANAGEMENT

The most dramatic and far-reaching development within the health care system during the last fifteen years has been the emergence of "multi-institutional systems," a broad term that describes a variety of collaborative arrangements between health care facilities.[32] Some of the most common of these arrangements include shared services, multi-hospital systems, and contract management. The emergence of such arrangements has included the development of numerous businesses, service groups, and professional groups that constitute strong, new economic interests in the health care sector.

Within these categories there are great variations. For example, a number of facilities might share services that include purchasing (the most common), data processing, and clinical services. The latter is the slowest-growing element in this category.[33]

Through shared services hospitals hope to achieve economies of scale and to secure group discounts on purchasing. Scott S. Parker, President of the Associated Hospital System, a "super" purchasing and shared services group, for example, estimated that his group would purchase $250 million in hospital supplies and $100 million in equipment in 1979. The purchases would be made at very advantageous rates. Parker reported that his company had contracted to buy $16 million worth of pharmaceuticals from more than thirty suppliers at a 25 percent aggregate discount.[34]

These purchasing companies not only control large amounts of capital, but they have formed working relationships with other powerful corporations. For example, the Sun Alliance in Charlotte, North Carolina, signed purchasing agreements with five suppliers—Sears Roebuck and Co.; Curtin-Matheson; Technicon Corporation; Amsco, Inc.; and Sechrest Industries—for $3 million worth of equipment.[35]

Multi-hospital systems are networks of health care facilities under one management system, which may only manage the constituent facilities or may own them as well. These systems may manage either for-profit or non-profit hospitals. They enjoyed great growth during the 1970's. As of August 1979, about 1,772 hospitals (30 percent of non-federal, short-term acute care institutions) were in multi-hospitals systems. This was a 21 percent increase over 1975.[36]

Vast sums of capital are expended in creating these multi-hospital systems. They are formed either through purchase or expansion of existing facilities or through the construction of new ones. There is an abundance of "acquisition opportunities" for buyers "with almost 300 hospitals on the block." Included in this group are certain relatively new proprietary hospitals, being sold for tax reasons or "because their owners are concerned about increasing government regulation," and old city- and county-owned hospitals that need replacement. Neither the municipalities nor the taxpayers want to pay for new facilities.[37]

Humana, Inc., "the nation's first billion dollar hospital company," provides an example of the scope of these operations. Between 1968 and 1978, Humana "built, acquired or leased 60 hospitals with 8,507 beds." In September 1978 Humana took over Medicorp, "which owned or leased 7,838 hospital beds in 13 states." David A. Jones, Chairman and Chief Executive Officer for Humana, as well as its co-founder, says, "Humana is spending more than $150 million to expand its successful hospitals, because 'That's our best opportunity'. The next best opportunity for growth is the construction of new facilities."[38] Thus Humana aims to increase the number of hospital beds, not decrease them, a goal that runs against the policies of both industry and government planners. John B. Hayes of the Nashville-based securities firm of J. C. Bradford and Company "estimates that in fiscal 1979 Humana's average return on common shareholders' equity jumped to 24 percent from a 19 percent return in fiscal 1978. This profitability is expected to improve because the average occupancy of its hospitals is "low at around 57% of licensed beds." The national average is around 75 percent. The low occupancy rate is attributed to the fact that Humana's hospitals are relatively new; "11 were opened in 1977 alone." Although it takes about eighteen months for a new hospital to break even, according to Jones, less than 5 percent of Humana's hospitals are losing money.[39]

Considering the facts that empty hospital beds are so expensive to maintain and that all attempts to contain hospital costs have involved attempts to reduce their numbers, the ability of Humana to realize profits and expand with a 57 percent occupancy rate is remarkable. One possible explanation lies in the patient markets toward which Humana is directed. Humana has been selling off its least profitable units and is attempting to "grow the charge side of the business." The charge side includes patients who pay their own bills or are covered by third-party payers "that pay what hospitals charge versus payers such as Medicare and Medicaid, which pay less than the full cost of caring for patients." In order to do this, Humana aims at increasing utilization of Humana's units by patients and doctors who are now using competing facilities. This contributes to a cycle in which hospitals with large numbers of poor patients are losing their paying patients to hospitals in multi-systems and are gradually being forced out of business. As they close, the medically indigent are left with no place to go, thus effectively reducing health care costs for the nation, as well as access to medical facilities by the poor.

Part of Humana's marketing strategy includes attempts to form coalitions with other powerful groups, including industry. According to Wendell Cherry, co-founder of Humana, the company is "trying to find out if there could be larger alliances—possibly more direct relations with employer and employee groups." To accomplish that goal, the company attempts to "determine how its hospitals can help patients' employers manage their group health insurance programs."[40]

Humana attributes its profitability to lower-than-average expenses due to its capacity to keep down construction and labor costs. The company has been sensitive to this issue, since its administrators realize that a number of interested groups are concerned about the impact Humana will have on health care costs—groups such as "taxpayers, government officials, patients and third-party payers." On the other hand, Humana's investors are looking for profits. Cherry reports that Humana has solved this "marketing problem" by building hospitals "for about 30% below the national average costs." In addition, the company has kept its labor costs to 34–36 percent of total costs; the national average is 51 percent.[41] These lower construction and labor costs are explained in part by the fact that multihospitals in general, including Humana, have been most successful in the Sun Belt, in areas where new industry was moving in during the 1970's and populations were growing. These locations meet all the requirements for the establishment of alternative health care delivery: they have large populations of employed people with young families who do not have established ties with the traditional sys-

tem. Multi-hospitals in such areas are thus able to attract disproportionate numbers of patients who either can afford to pay their
own bills or are covered by adequate third-party insurance arrangements. In places where these conditions do not hold and where external controls threaten it's profitability, Humana has eliminated some
of its holdings. For example, the corporation sold its properties in
New Jersey when the state adopted the super-rational diagnosis related group reimbursement mechanism in the attempt to control
health care costs. Industry, of course, supports the DRGs.

The effect of multi-hospitals, such as Humana, on the structure
of health care delivery would be to increase the number of patients
served by self-paying and private third-party systems and to decrease, in the absence of facilities, the number of indigent patients
and those served by Medicare and Medicaid. The long-range effect
would be a strong contribution to the reversal of the social welfare
trend in medicine that has continued since the 1930's, thus con-
tributing to greater inequalities in medical services to consumers. In
short, Humana represents a return to laissez-faire in the health care
system. It also represents implementation of some managerial efficiencies, which may result in greater profits for their stockholders.
There is no evidence, however, that they lead to reductions in health
care costs. In fact, the *Wall Street Journal* reports that a study published in 1983 "suggests that the big, for-profit chains apparently
make much of their money by performing more extensive services,
charging higher prices and more aggressively collecting bills than
do nonprofit institutions."[42]

In addition to shared services and multi-hospital systems, contract management has become an important form of collaborative
arrangement. It involves management by an outside organization of
one or more departments within a facility that maintains its own
autonomy. This service may be delivered by a hospital, a consulting
firm, or a multi-hospital management system that has "unbundled"
its services. Unbundling, which is a relatively new development,
means the selling of only part of the total management package rather
than taking over and coordinating the entire institution, as multi-
hospitals have insisted on doing in the past.[43]

These arrangements were virtually unknown before the passage
of Medicare. By 1975 the trend in this direction had been well documented. Taylor, for instance, has reported an increase of 218 per-

cent in the number of hospitals sharing purchasing services between 1970 and 1975, as well as the addition of new shared clinical services.[44] In 1979 he reported that hospitals had both continued and increased their participation in shared services programs.[45]

Multi-institutional systems are enormously complex organizations; an analysis of them is outside the scope of this study. Yet for our purposes multi-systems are important because of two categories of questions they raise. First, why did they appear? What were the conditions for their development and continued growth? Second, how does their emergence affect the traditional practice of medicine? In particular, how do they affect the division of authority between physicians and administrators within the health care system?

GROWTH AND DEVELOPMENT OF
MULTI-INSTITUTIONALS

The emergence and growth of collaborative ventures in the health care system are usually attributed to four factors. First, they are stimulated by regulatory pressures from various sources that encourage and sometimes mandate such agreements. For example, Barrett notes that in Massachusetts, HSA number IV required that all hospitals be part of a multi-hospital system by 1980.[46] Planning arrangements seem very conducive to the development of multi-units.

Modern Healthcare reports that not only are HSAs being encouraged to facilitate the development of multi-unit relationships within their regions, but "certificate-of-need and rate-review legislation are expected to provide similar encouragements during the next five years, all under the influence of the national health priorities of P.L. 93–641."[47]

Second, dramatic increases in operating costs have forced some facilities to collaborate as a condition for survival.

Third, capital for construction and equipment has become more difficult and more expensive to acquire. Both private donors and lending institutions, often under pressures from area HSAs, are reluctant to provide capital unless need is clearly demonstrated. This is in part a result of some of the community activism advocated by industry, which was described in chapter 5.

Fourth, consumers both are more vocal in demanding health care and are more sophisticated in evaluating it. One reason for this increased consumer sophistication is the fact that corporate employers are now grouped into the consumer category, another relatively new development. Demands and evaluations by corporate consumers carry far more weight than do those of private citizens or consumer groups whose resources for input are relatively limited.

Of these four factors credited with the emergence of multi-institutional arrangements, all were either events that stimulated industry's interest in the health care system (early regulation to provide access, which stimulated legislation to control access and insure quality; rapidly increasing costs; and inflation associated with tight, expensive capital) or are caused in part by industry's intervention in the system (pressure from planning agencies and, more directly, from consumers themselves, including industry.) In fact, it is often stated in the provider press that government and private sector leaders in health care see multi-unit hospital systems as sources of cost containment.[48]

Once they emerge as a result of these structural supports, multi-hospitals are by definition structurally supported; this contributes to their continuing development. For example, Brown reports that

shared service organizations acquired a new institutional membership category in the American Hospital Association and the AHA also announced establishment of a Panel on Multihospital Systems in January. By the end of the year, the AHA had established a Center for Multi-Institutional Systems, which is to be headed by Robert E. Toomey, a foremost advocate of this structure. With this type of national recognition, discussions on multi-institutional arrangements can now, it seems, be expected to show up in commission reports, planning documents, speeches, and other areas in which newly established and accepted ideas get repeated.[49]

In addition to these new institutional membership categories, the American Hospital Association contributes to the development of multi-hospitals in other ways. The AHA Center for Smaller and Rural Hospitals is chaired by Derek Bush, who said the center "encourages their 2000 plus constituency to develop and join multihospital systems."[50] Brown and McCool report that most national and state professional organizations recognize this growth and encourage it.

The AHA is mounting a campaign to recruit investor-owned multi-hospitals into its membership. One recruitment strategy is to give the multi-hospital a discount on dues, so that the aggregate dues of one system's members do not exceed those paid by single hospital members.[51]

The AHA is aiming to recruit investor-owned chains in particular, because, according to David G. Williamson, Jr.,[52] member of the AHA advisory panel on dues/multi-institutional arrangements, it is thought that such membership would "give the Association more clout in dealing with Congress and federal agencies."[53] In this way the AHA and multi-hospitals form a coalition in which each supports increased power for the other. This is a new coalition within the health care system itself, which increases the power of administrators and managers at the expense of professional authority.

The investor-owned hospital industry has surged into prominence over the last fifteen years. According to a report from Frost and Sullivan, "Nothing short of seizure by the federal government can have a serious effect on their operations." The assets of this industry are now 5.6 percent of the assets of all U.S. non-federal acute care hospitals, as opposed to 2.5 percent ten years ago.[54]

This controversy points up the increasing competition between investor-owned and non-profit multi-systems. As the financial squeeze is put on public hospitals, their share of the market declines while the private market expands. Lloyd L. Cannedy, who was named Young Hospital Administrator of the Year by the American College of Hospital Administrators in 1979, describes a cycle in which public hospitals lose their most profitable patients to for-profit hospitals.[55] Bad debts increase, forcing these institutions into ever worse financial conditions: "This happens because a decline in a local government hospital's market share means that other hospitals are expanding with new facilities that attract patients." The result is that public hospitals are left with indigent patients and bad debts, which may ultimately force them to close.[56]

Perrow describes the cycle in much the same terms. Proprietary hospitals, which are usually owned by a group of physicians or a franchising chain and operate for a profit, "spring up and take the profitable cases. . . . the voluntary hospital is left with the complex, expensive cases that need expensive stand-by facilities, the charity cases, and the long-term patients who require expensive care."[57]

The effect of this particular rationalization is to insure that treatment will be withdrawn from the members of the hospital population that is least profitable precisely because they need care the most, while services proliferate for those who are most profitable.

As a result of regulatory pressures and economic and organizational processes, for-profit hospital chains have grown rapidly and are now one of the hottest items on the stock market.

Leading, publicly owned, proprietary hospital management companies will post hefty earnings increases and substantial revenue gains in 1980, security analysts predict. . . . Regulation pressure from federal agencies will force more and more hospitals to seek help from multi-hospital systems, boosting the latter's profits, analysts believe. The industry's profit outlook is also boosted by management companies' good image in the money markets. Thus, hospital management companies can attract long-term financing when money is tight better than companies in other industries, analysts believe.[58]

Some of the effects these developments have on health care delivery are exemplified by events in kidney dialysis. When the federal government tightened federal reimbursement regulations for this treatment, it increased the development of new contract management services in this area. In the past, hospitals have been able to win preferential reimbursement exceptions for themselves, which are now being eliminated to "provide monetary incentives for efficient operations." As a result of these pressures, some hospitals have stopped offering dialysis treatment and many others will be reassessing their programs. *Modern Healthcare* reported in 1980 that Larry M. Day, President of Dialysis Management, Inc., Littleton, Colorado, created his company in 1979 in anticipation of the federal reimbursement plan. Day criticized hospital-based dialysis programs claiming they were "inefficient" because "hospital administrators and financial managers [had] relinquished management control of the units almost totally to medical and technical staff because of the 'mystique' that surrounds the programs." The number of proprietary and non-profit free-standing dialysis programs had ballooned since 1973, when Medicare first started to cover the treatment. These units are usually not owned nor operated by hospitals. By 1980 there were about 280 of them, treating 47 percent of all dialysis patients. A single investor-owned firm in Boston, National Medical Care, operated 115. Once the firm was established, it began to lobby the government to establish one universal, prospective dialysis rate, which would increase reimbursements to the free-standing units and decrease those for hospitals. "Companies like National Medical Care, which is expecting about $200 million in revenues this year [1980], have shown that dialysis treatment can be profitable."[59]

This push to establish a standard, basic dialysis rate might have had additional effects. It might have used government regulation to sustain and enhance the positions of privately owned, free-standing units, which they claimed to have achieved in the first place through competitive economies. The rates that the units were paid would then have been pushed up, making them less economical. Hospitals, in the meantime, would increasingly have been pushed out of the field. This is the familiar process that has caused health care regulations to function in the interest of other commercial interests.

However, in 1983 under the Reagan administration Health and Human Services (HHS) foresaw this possibility and headed it off with payment changes in the Medicare End Stage Renal Dialysis Program. In 1982 Medicare paid an estimated $170 for each dialysis treatment delivered in a hospital and about $138 for those in free-standing units. The new prospective reimbursement fees would be fixed at about $131 for most hospitals, adjusting for regional differences, and $127 for free-standing units. HHS estimates it currently costs $97 a treatment to dialyze at home. It is attempting to encourage home dialysis by setting fixed physician fees. Medicare now pays an average of $200 a month to doctors for each patient on hospital or free-standing dialysis. For home dialysis the average fee is $150. HHS wants to pay a fixed physician fee of $184 no matter where dialysis is done.[60] These fixed rates favor the development of free-standing units over hospitals and home-based dialysis over either of the other two.

In terms of profits, of course, if hospitals were successfully driven from the field, patients would have no alternative to the free-standing units. It is believed that hospitals treat older, sicker dialysis patients. Presumably the profitable, free-standing units would not wish to treat them, since to do so either would diminish cost-efficiency through increased utilization or would raise the units' mortality statistics. Again it appears that their profitability is at least in part the result of having skimmed off the elite of the kidney dialysis population. Its effect is to create a new private sector of capitalist medicine.

MULTI-INSTITUTIONAL ARRANGEMENTS

Where multi-institutional systems develop, they alter the balance of power between physicians and administrators. This is so for a number of reasons.

First, the size and complexity of the multi-units diminish the role of physicians within any given facility. The size of the operation demands sophisticated managerial apparatus. The importance of complex management, combined with the increasingly foggy boundaries between professional and administrative responsibility, insures a growth in the power of administrators over physicians.

The complexity of the systems contributes more than this. Administrators of individual hospitals in multi-hospital systems lose power themselves as their price of entry into the multi-system. This means that even if they wished to maintain the traditional coalition between physicians and administrators in hospitals, they would be unable to do so. This is a major component of the process through which multi-institutions emerge in the health care system, while the traditional, physician-centered system declines; they are two sides of the same coin.

In multi-hospitals, basic decisions are made at the larger, higher management level by individuals with no close working ties with physicians and little interest in the competitive position of any particular hospital in relation to another.

With the growth of boards and administrators of hospitals who are increasingly willing to relinquish hospital autonomy as a condition of survival and as the price of membership in powerful coalitions, the physicians servicing them will be less able to improve their own status through capital purchases or construction of individual hospitals to which they are allocated.

This analysis of the physicians' role is reflected throughout the literature on multi-hospital systems. The following statement by Brown and McCool provides an example:

In multihospital systems, the relative power of the medical staff is lessened somewhat as corporate boards and officers have more control over individual institutions. The physicians remain the most important customers, but they cannot impose projects on the organization without a sound marketing assessment as they often can in single hospitals.[61]

Brown and McCool also point out that in this sense multi-hospital systems function much like HMOs. The multi-hospitals could very easily become HMOs, in fact. Thus, Brown and McCool predict that as HMOs gain strength in the marketplace, putting pressure on more traditional delivery systems, all types of chains will be ready to join the trend and offer the HMO option.[62] This clarifies the issue raised as to why industry would define profit-making multi-hospitals as cost-efficient. Actually, they are rationalizing mechanisms that can and will respond to competitive pressures from HMOs even as they apply pressures to the more traditional system. They might be viewed as an interim stage in the transition of the health care system, forms that can survive only as long as they are competitive. That is, multi-hospitals are viewed as competitive to the traditional system but not necessarily to HMOs, which industry favors.

For the moment multi-hospitals can be seen to have many of the professional control mechanisms of HMOs, including, very importantly, peer and utilization review. Mendenco, Inc., Houston (now Lifemark), is a multi-hospital system that has implemented standardized "quality assurance" activities for the sixteen hospitals it owns or leases and is considering marketing its quality assurance consulting services to non-Mendenco hospitals. The company has assigned special staff to coordinate eight programs, five of which center around the control and accountability of physicians.[63]

In addition to physician controls as a result of multi-hospital systems, other collaborative arrangements also affect physician practices and prestige. For example, Larry Day of Dialysis Management, Inc., speaks in an obviously disparaging way of the inefficiency resulting from control over dialysis programs by medical and technical staff.

As part of the process of constructing new collaborative arrangements, older practices and agreements have come to be redefined. For example, Dean Grant states that the contracts that hospitals negotiate with individuals or groups of physicians to provide specific diagnostic, therapeutic, and clinical services, as well as to provide medical supervision in their departments, are now "being recognized for what they are—a special form of 'unbundled' contract managements service." In 1979, 5 percent of every health care dollar spent was used to pay for these services, over $7 billion annually. These contracts represent 7–9 percent of the total operating budgets of hospitals. (This sum does not include fees paid by physicians often based in hospitals, such as anesthesiologists and radiologists, because they bill hospital patients directly.) Grant notes with disapproval that as recently as 1977 less than half of these arrangements involved written agreements: "A gentlemen's agreement seems hardly appropriate for an arrangement that could cost a hospital over $1 million annually."[64]

Because of pressure from consumers and government regulators, including attempts by state rate review agencies to obtain authority to review hospital-based physician fees as a hospital cost, Grant reports that there has been a move by physicians' groups to change their current contracts to provide for direct billing arrangements. They want to separate themselves from the hospitals in order to minimize hospital influence over the physicians' practices and fees. This will be far more difficult for some kinds of specialties than others. Pathologists, for example, would have to direct bill for 250,000–300,000 minor procedures.[65]

Physicians have also attempted to protect their prerogatives by formalizing their contracts, a move that is approved by both physicians and hospitals. Some physicians fear that government regulations might begin to define exactly how they will be reimbursed. The specialty medical societies wish to protect their members' professional rights and financial arrangements by negotiating long-term contracts with hospitals.[66]

This is not a generalized fear of wage controls but, Grant maintains, is stimulated by such rulings as that of the original 1964 Medicare regulation, which withholds reimbursement for services that do not directly involve a physician. This ruling can have very far-reaching effects on pathologists, for whom "such services represent about 85% of . . . traditional compensation."[67]

The administrator is motivated to renegotiate, if possible, or at least to formalize physician contracts by pressures from a number of areas, including the Health Care Financing Administration, state rate review agencies, and the public. "Some unique contracts have yielded extraordinary compensation levels ($400,000 and up) that when publicized were embarrassing to hospital managers and trustees."[68] To comply with the Medicare regulation would require that administrators state explicitly what percentage of the physicians' remuneration is allocated for "administrative and supervisory" functions. Grant asks rhetorically:

how will a governing board react when an administrator reports that the hospital is officially sanctioning $150,000 or more of the pathologists' compensation as purely "administrative and supervisory," as Part A requires. Is this reasonable compensation for administrative functions? Also, will Medicare consider this an unreasonable cost? Is the hospital acting as a prudent buyer in the purchase of high-priced lab administrators?[69]

This rationalized process of rate evaluation and record keeping erodes the power of physicians to maintain control over information concerning the economic aspects of their work or the actual nature of the work they do. Such processes increase the extent to which physicians are visibly subjected to bureaucratic accountability. Moreover, even if the physicians' attempts to control information were to succeed, their negotiations, record keeping, and administration of payments procedures would place them in the position of becoming mere businessmen, managers and bureaucrats of their own accounts, making it harder to maintain their self and public images as professional-scientists.

Physicians' groups, unlike other medical service contractors, are usually individual local groups rather than large nationwide corporations that serve several hundred hospitals. Thus they are not equipped to deal with multi-local, multi-hospital systems.

Emergency care specialists may become an exception. Thus, according to Grant, "they are emerging as large, well organized corporations serving regional and national markets. Consequently, emergency groups offer more competitive and consistent contractual terms."[70] They are still another category of physicians that has emerged whose interests and practices are antithetical to those of traditional practitioners.

Some providers are advocating another alternative method of organization to these voluntary and investor-owned multi-hospitals. Physicians could organize themselves "vertically" with university teaching hospitals forming their anchors. These vertical systems would consist of coordinated complementary institutions, that is, hospitals, nursing homes, or hospitals with ambulatory facilities. They would consist of hospitals and ancillary services, including private practicing physicians.[71]

In an interview with *Modern Healthcare*, Dr. James A. Campbell, head of the only well-developed vertically integrated system in the United States, the Rush-Presbyterian-St. Luke's Medical Center in Chicago, expressed the opinion that if physicians do not form such networks voluntarily, they could be forced to do so. He stated that "the industry already has been enticed and regulated into emergency medical service networks, end-stage renal networks, cancer control networks, area health education centers and maternal and neonatal care networks." As a result of (1) new regulations, (2) competition from "horizontally organized" (the sharing, cooperation, coordination, or merger of like institutions), multi-hospital systems, (3) controls on the introduction of new medical technology and services, and (4) changes in the structure of the health care market, the viability of free-standing medical centers, including those belonging to medical schools, is increasingly threatened.[72]

Campbell proposes that 120–150 university-based systems such as the one he heads should be formed to link tertiary hospitals, academic centers, nursing homes, mental health facilities, home care, and primary care clinics, including health maintenance organizations and fee-for-service medical clinics. These systems should each serve their fair share of patients from various ethnic backgrounds, ages, income groups, and diagnostic categories.[73]

To date, this option does not appear to have been achieved to any high degree. However, another smaller rationalization process has been proceeding in at least one area of care—emergency room services. Duane Houtz, President of the American Hospital Association's Council on Ambulatory, Emergency and Home Healthcare, estimates that about half the country's hospitals have been active in categorization programs designed to ensure that emergency patients are directed to hospitals that can most effectively meet their medical needs. Both hospitals and physicians have resisted this move, because neither wished to be categorized permanently into a subordinate position within an emergency services network. However, the Joint Commission on Accreditation of Hospitals (JCAH) contributed to the breakdown of that resistance through implementation (in January 1979) of new emergency service standards. These standards designate four levels of emergency care "I (comprehensive) through IV (first aid/referral) to identify hospitals' emergency service capabilities. The standards require that hospitals promote, develop and implement a community-based emergency plan and that they classify themselves with the JCAH categories or a state or regional classifying system."[74]

SUMMARY

Throughout the Series industry has promoted initiatives for intervention in the health care sector that were intended simultaneously to cut immediate costs and to restructure the health care system to make it more cost-efficient in the long run. Once the system is restructured, according to this plan, market mechanisms will insure that it functions in a cost-efficient way and external regulation and controls will be unnecessary. A number of developments in health care organization look like responses to those initiatives. Changes have occurred at several levels.

First, physicians and hospitals have been forced into a defensive posture, as manifested by the Voluntary Effort. In an attempt to avoid additional regulations and controls, providers are attempting to undertake self-regulation, often utilizing the same processes and techniques advocated by industry. In doing so, they acknowledge the complaints of government, consumer groups, and industry.

Although industry does not support the VE unless it is directed toward restructuring the system, the effort acknowledges the ideological thrust of industry and works in the direction of industry's goals. Because providers have consistently denied that implementation of the VE cuts the quality of care, their efforts and even their successes constitute both evidence and acknowledgment that past services have been inefficiently organized, as industry has maintained. These processes give support to the idea that more effective administration is needed to override administrative control by physicians, who are allegedly either uninterested, incompetent, or too intent on their own economic or career interests to function in the interests of society. The VE also constitutes acceptance of the basic idea that industry has been trying to promulgate that was previously odious to providers: that cost considerations as well as patient welfare should influence diagnostic and treatment decisions.

The development of multi-institutional arrangements is enormously important in the health care system. Although they embody many of the processes industry advocates for rationalizing health care,

they are not directed toward decreasing health care services, facilities, or utilization for those who can afford to pay. Even those who
do not believe health care costs are too high and are not in favor of
such reductions agree that reducing utilization is the only way to
lower costs in the long run.

Multi-hospital systems cream off private patients and fully insured subscribers to prepaid medical plans, leaving the burden of
caring for the chronically ill, the aged, and the poor to public institutions and to partial payment systems. They do so at a time when
demands for cost cutting affect those institutions whose costs are
high in part because they deal with high-cost patients. In effect, the
multi-hospital alternative supports a new centralized bureaucratic,
commercial medical system.

Whether or not they prove cost-efficient in the long run, multi-
institutional arrangements facilitate the development of market
mechanisms as opposed to professional control; and planning is as
important in the marketplace as it is in establishing government
regulations. Rationalization is the heart of both processes. The development of multi-institutions simultaneously forces and institutionalizes physician subordination to bureaucratic planning and authority, whether governmental or business. By the time all possible
savings have been realized by cutting services for the poor, by
standardizing services, procedures, and equipment, and by enjoying
economies of scale, physicians may be firmly locked into the bureaucratic hierarchy without the structural mechanisms required to
support either their claims for professionalism or their self-images
as professionals.

7

Conclusions

Since the early 1970's qualitative changes have occurred within the structure of the American health care system that have been both a cause and a consequence of a transformation in the occupational authority enjoyed by physicians. The image and ideology of the independent, free professional whose decisions are grounded in technical knowledge and the service ethic are giving way to the intrusion into medicine of managerial accountability and control.

These changes have been the result of qualities not of either professionalism or bureaucratic management themselves but of complex events in the larger social environment. Most importantly, they have been facilitated by the strategic activities of American corporations intent on restructuring and rationalizing health care delivery in an attempt to cut costs. These strategies have been designed to remove the historic social supports upon which the occupational power of physicians has been structured and to replace them with supports for new authority arrangements as an essential requisite of the transformation.

This study has focused on changes in health care structure since the early 1970's because it was at this point that industry's strategy was launched. But the roots of the contemporary health care system go back to the late 1930's, when government first began enacting legislation designed to increase access to health services for the poor through Social Security amendments, to aid construction of additional treatment facilities through the Hill-Burton Act, and to facil-itate the development of health insurance plans through passage of Blue Cross-enabling legislation.

Although physicians opposed many of them, these developments did not themselves challenge the legitimacy of professional power; in fact, they almost certainly increased it. These were the founda-tions upon which emerged an extremely rich and powerful health care system. Because the knowledge and service claims of profes-sionals remained unquestioned through this process, and perhaps because no one saw any immediate advantage in attempting to dis-lodge them, physicians functioned as the natural rulers of what was becoming a vast new empire.

It was not until the mid–1960's, when the socialization of health care reached its zenith, manifested in the concrete provisions of Medicare and Medicaid, that a challenge to physicians' claims that their decisions were based on knowledge and the service ethic was launched. The bureaucratic and regulatory apparatus established by Medicaid and Medicare, although it was never used effectively by government, was a crucial tool for industry in its attempts to gain control over physicians. Completely new structural forms began to appear rapidly after the mid–1960's. Those which proved most useful in limiting professional authority and control include the following.

REIMBURSEMENT MECHANISMS, POLICIES, AND REGULATIONS

From the mid–1940's until the mid–1960's, increasing numbers of people were guaranteed certain health services under third-party payment systems, first private insurance and then Medicare and Medicaid. Most of these early plans covered only treatments within hospitals, where utilization rates soared. The national bill for health care rose rapidly, especially after passage of Medicare and Medicaid. Attempts to control utilization and, therefore, costs resulted in pas-sage of peer and utilization review legislation by the federal govern-ment and in the emergence of a complex structure of peer standards review organizations. This apparatus has been used extensively by corporations and private insurance carriers to do peer and utiliza-tion review for privately insured patients and for all kinds of treat-ment and diagnostic procedures in both hospitals and ambulatory care facilities.

Third-party payment programs and the peer and utilization review apparatus that has developed around them have become extremely complex, competitive, and diverse. Within these structures exist many individual and group interests that are antithetical to physician dominance within the health care system. These include supporters and beneficiaries of stringent federal regulation and control programs both within and outside government agencies; corporate employers who wish to meet their negotiated obligations to provide health insurance benefits to employees as cheaply as possible; many different varieties of insurance carriers who, as the price of competitive survival, are motivated to meet utilization and cost control demands of corporate consumers; and the consumers of health care services themselves, who are interested in peer and utilization review both to reduce costs, which they perceive themselves to be paying through increased premiums, inflation, and decreased wage packages, and to avoid costly and sometimes dangerous unnecessary treatments.

These pressures have resulted in divisions between providers. Physicians themselves are divided among those who work in or through review boards, thus benefiting from regulation, and those who do not. Physicians and hospital administrators are divided and their historical coalition undermined by the fact that hospitals must meet cost control demands of outside parties as a price of continuing survival. Hospitals must enforce regulations whether physicians like it or not.

Federal occupational and environmental health-related legislation such as the Occupational Safety and Health Act and the Toxic Substances Control Act have stimulated developments that also threaten physician autonomy and authority.

First, regulations require that employees exposed to certain hazardous substances or conditions in their workplaces be informed of that fact and provided with free, periodic health care examinations. Some corporations have established their own industrial health programs in order to comply with that regulation as economically as possible. This has further increased the numbers of employed, supervised, and accountable physicians; stimulated the development of occupational medicine as a specialty; and, to some extent, made the plant rather than the hospital, clinic, or doctor's office the center for health care delivery.

Second, corporations are required to collect and provide the federal government with data that indicate that certain substances or procedures are hazardous to health. Corporations have historically been interested in occupational health research and have attempted to control it in their own interests, as in the case of asbestos and asbestos-related industries. Occupational physicians working in plants will play an important role in collecting data concerning occupational diseases among employees that may be used to set new or more stringent safety standards; legitimating whatever levels are set; and maintaining control of potentially damaging data by claiming doctor-patient confidentiality to resist relinquishing it.

Industry has anticipated these developments and has increased the numbers of industry-based training programs for occupational physicians; at the same time, academically based programs have declined. Industry may thus maintain control of this occupational specialty through educational programs as well as through its power as the employer of the occupational physician.

Industry has been concerned with upgrading the status and prestige of occupational medicine, which have historically been low. Although a major reason for this has been the often voiced suspicion that the company doctor was more concerned with the welfare of employers than that of patients, industry blames the medical profession itself for the low status of this specialty. In this view, professionally controlled medical schools have conducted insufficient or inadequate training programs for occupational medicine and have forbidden the treatment by company doctors of any condition that was not work-related in order to protect their own narrow economic interests.

Some in industry have begun to counter-attack, claiming that, because of their poor training in the area, private practitioners are incompetent to recognize or treat work-caused illnesses. This constitutes a direct attack on both the professional knowledge base and the professional control of the educational system.

ALTERNATIVE HEALTH CARE SETTINGS

Two major, new kinds of delivery systems function to enforce peer and utilization review procedures and increase cost-efficiency. First, alternative treatment settings, such as out-patient clinics and surgi-centers, have increased in numbers. These facilities exercise more stringent peer and utilization reviews and employ larger numbers of paraprofessionals than are found in the traditional system. They simultaneously compete with traditional service and provide nontraditional, controlled work settings for physicians, who are thus socialized to new work habits. Hospitals are increasingly forced to adopt their management techniques and strategies in order to survive the competition. Sometimes they are unable to do so and are forced to abandon the delivery of certain services; for example, some hospitals are closing their kidney dialysis units.

Second, the development of health maintenance organizations seems directly related to the control of hospital utilization and, therefore, costs. HMOs force administrative controls on physicians even when they are physician owned and operated as the price of economic survival. Such is the case with IPA-HMOs.

HMOs are capable of the most far-reaching kind of control, ranging from initial planning and allocations of facilities, supplies, and personnel to day-by-day supervision over all diagnostic and treatment procedures. The medical profession has opposed HMOs historically but in the past few years has shown more acceptance.

HEALTH CARE PLANNING

The federal government attempted to introduce planning into the health care system with a number of different pieces of legislation, none of which challenged traditional professional authority or contained sanctioning mechanisms.

By far the most effective piece of planning legislation has been the industry-supported National Health Planning and Resources Development Act of 1974, which provided for the development of a national network of regional health systems agencies, on whose boards consumer majorities are mandated. Industry has encouraged and trained executives to serve on these boards and to take a far more active, critical role than they have done in the past.

The act also provided for a certificate of need program that attempted to slow the growth of health care facilities and the acquisition of expensive, high-technology capital equipment. Industry believes physicians utilize this equipment unnecessarily in order to pay for it and as part of the practice of defensive medicine.

Industry supported the planning act initially and has done political work for amendments extending its regulatory powers. Thus industry's positions have been consistently in direct opposition to those taken by the AMA.

Industry has also supported the health system agencies in its own regions, both through direct participation by executives as consumer members of their boards and through financial assistance. Industry has used its economic power over insurance carriers to enforce HSA rulings through reimbursement policies, as, for example, by refusing to pay for procedures done using equipment or facilities not approved by the regional HSA. These developments make physicians increasingly accountable to bureaucratic managers and planners. As these external pressures have built, the traditional health care delivery system has made a number of adaptive responses, including radical changes in management practices and physician behavior.

MULTI-INSTITUTIONAL SYSTEMS

During the last decade there has been a proliferation of various kinds of multi-institutional managerial and purchasing arrangements by hospitals. These range in complexity from group buying contracts to vast, multi-hospital systems run by billion-dollar consulting firms. In terms of health services planning and cost-efficiency through control of physician decision making, these systems function in much the same way as do HMOs, to which they could easily be converted.

Multi-systems function outside the traditional physician-administrator coalitions. They are almost completely controlled by management experts who make their decisions on the basis of their assessments of developments in the health care marketplace. Planning is perhaps even more important to these managers than it is to government bureaucrats, who must often substitute political considerations for the bottom line. Rationalization is inherent in multi-institutional systems, which simultaneously force and institutionalize physician subordination to bureaucratic planning and authority.

As these new structural mechanisms proliferate, they contain their own interest groups and legitimating mechanisms, which are competitive and antithetical to professional interests and legitimations. The probability that they are also stronger and more congruent with contemporary reality is evidenced by the fact that physicians have been forced to tolerate and work within them.

An inherent assumption underlying all these new structural forms is that physicians must be made accountable to those who use and pay for health care services. The demands for accountability and the structural forms for achieving it emerged almost simultaneously. Medicare and Medicaid had hardly passed, expanding access to health care for the poor and elderly, before further amendments to the Social Security Act were made that were designed to limit it again. These were the peer and utilization review and the fraud and abuse amendments. Rather than attack the ideology of health care as a social right, these amendments attempted to force physicians to limit access to the system, probably a safer political move. However, the attempt itself contained the inherent assumption that physicians had been abusing the system. They thus constituted an essential attack on the legitimating ideology underlying physician authority, the claim that treatment and diagnostic decisions are based purely on concern for the welfare of the patient, the service ethic.

Although the language of this attack defined the problem as unnecessary or abusive utilization, the way regulatory controls have been used makes it clear that the aim is the restructuring of medical decision-making authority. Thus utilization review, which was originally intended to reduce unnecessary hospitalization for publicly funded patients, has been expanded to cover all treatment and diagnostic procedures for both publicly and privately funded patients in both in- and out-patient facilities. This expanded interpretation does not come from government regulations, however, but from initiatives taken by industry, which makes use of those regulations. It is in the Series where demands for professional accountability are loudest and criticism of professional ethics as a control mechanism is most harsh, not in government regulations.

The Series attacks the knowledge base of physicians as well as the service ethic. For example, it points out that traditional practitioners treat illness, rather than maintaining health; that they rely on community standards rather than empirical evidence of the efficacy of treatments; and that they are ignorant of good diagnostic and treatment procedures for occupational disease.

The Series also undermines the belief that a special relationship exists between physicians and their patients, advocating the use of nurses for functions physicians have filled in the past, not just as a cost-saving move but because nurses are seen as better in some way.

Conversely, the Series speaks often of the efficacy, rationality, and public spirit of corporate executives, management consultants, and business administrators who are striving to set the health care system on the right road, over the opposition of traditional physicians, hospital administrators, government officials under their influence, and the users of health care services who are in awe of their physicians. It thus promotes an ideology of managerial efficiency and accountability as a model for professional workers to follow.

This ideological rhetoric functions to legitimate more concrete developments undermining professional autonomy and authority. These developments take a number of forms.

Peer and utilization review in all kinds of health care settings, including HMOs, hospitals, and out-patient facilities, requires standards against which to evaluate practice patterns. But specific, universally accepted diagnostic and treatment standards have never existed in medical practice. Two techniques are now being used to set such standards.

The technique utilized by United States Administrators has been to use a select panel of physicians to set uniform standards against which the practices of all other physicians, nurses, and paraprofessionals can then be evaluated. This is a process through which professional work is bureaucratized internally. The extent to which these forms of standardization are determined by cost containment desires of industry is what determines the effectiveness of industry in controlling the medical delivery system. Those physicians who are willing to perform this service, those who are in favor of cost cutting, will be the ones hired to sit on the panels. The fact that they are physicians is irrelevant. Their essential function is to legitimate standardization and regulation.

The second technique, exemplified by Damm's system and utilized by United States Administrators in its second phase, is used by consultants, managers, and administrators of various sorts. Computers simultaneously set and enforce uniform standards on the basis of information about every aspect of health care that is collected and fed into them. This information includes the diagnostic and treatment patterns of individual physicians, the fees they charge, the numbers of times they call back patients, and the effectiveness of their treatments. The computer then works out averages, which become the new standards against which performance is measured.

Management circulates periodic reports to all physicians showing the utilization patterns of each individual. Usually it is not necessary to attempt to force compliance; as one hospital administrator puts it, "a natural convergence to the mean occurs." When it does not, sanctions may be utilized against the physicians involved. These range from withholding money from the offending physician to terminating him or her from the group. Thus the mere fact of working within some sort of group facilitates the control of professional workers.

These developments may or may not improve medical practice. They may certainly be expected to reduce the autonomy and decision-making authority of physicians. This statistical practice of medicine could function to reduce the use of informed judgements by physicians in their practices. To some extent, it removes uncertainty from the treatment situation, not because the doctor knows exactly what would work best with a given patient, but because he or she knows what the "average" decision would be. If Damm's dream of a totally rationalized health care system were to come true, the following of such an average course might protect the physician against a malpractice suit; conversely, failure to do so might cause such suits in the future, a possibility Damm does not discuss.

These statistical, computerized techniques represent the ultimate in purely formal—as opposed to cause-effect—rationality. The techniques are neutral in themselves and may be used to achieve the goals that are determined by those who control them and that may fall anywhere between the poles of maximizing health care and minimizing delivery costs. Within the health care system the new computer technology is increasingly used by managers, consultants, and insurance carriers of various sorts to control professional decision making; legitimate that control on the grounds of the rationality of the techniques; cut health care services and, thus, costs, without incurring a political reaction; and transform professionalism itself by denying the primacy of knowledge and service considerations in professional decision making in order to legitimate procedures to make the physician accountable.

Theorists such as Goss have argued from good evidence that when professionals and bureaucrats work in the same settings, parallel authority arrangements are the rule. Physicians may lose administrative but not technical authority. The first potential violation of that general rule was manifested by the adoption of utilization control. Initially, since it aimed only to prevent or reduce the lengths of hospital stays, the impact of these controls on professional decision making would have been minimal, had they been enforceable, which they were not.

Conformity is now enforced indirectly through the introduction of increased competition within the health care system. Those facilities that perform the least services have a competitive edge in a new health care environment, which stresses cost-efficiency as the ultimate value.

Techniques for diagnosing and treating minimal numbers of illnesses take two forms. One is stringent utilization review and control; the other is the selection of patient populations that are healthiest. The latter goal is achieved through certain structural characteristics of the health care system itself. For example, insurance plans, health maintenance organizations, and, increasingly, for-profit, multi-hospital systems siphon off working people with young families who have the lowest morbidity rates. Experience rating is used as a cost accounting principle by insurance companies, thereby increasing the cost of health care for those who need it most, the poor, sick and elderly. This effectively rations their use of medical care. Planning agency policies result in the location of facilities in such places and/or numbers as to reduce the possibility that certain groups will be diagnosed and treated. This is a result of the logic of maintaining hospitals in areas that are most profitable, rather than in areas of greatest need, and of limiting the facilities of service organizations, such as HMOs.

Where the technique for rationing services is utilization review, computers may check utilization of diagnostic tests and treatments, ranging from medication administered to surgeries performed, and compare the rates of each physician with those of the statistical averages. Some third-party payers refuse to reimburse for procedures that exceed those averages. Others utilize peer or managerial pressures to bring offenders into line.

In these cases it is clearly not gross abuses against which controls are aimed, but regulation of the most minute, everyday practice of medicine: diagnosis and treatment. This kind of control is intended both to cut costs and to establish administrative authority over the physician's practice. These goals are restated throughout the Series. The need to accomplish them is unquestioned and thus forms the background assumptions on which peer and utilization review and the statistical computerized techniques for carrying it out are constructed.

PHYSICIAN DEFENSES AGAINST EXTERNAL CONTROLS

Historically physicians and their professional associations have fought all attempts by outsiders to intervene in the health care system in any way. They fought every kind of government health care program and regulation, the creation of Blue Cross, and occupational health programs that showed any sign of impinging on private practice.

The physicians' battle against outside intervention in health care has taken four major forms. First, they opposed the passage of any legislation that would affect health care delivery. Second, when it was impossible for them to prevent passage, physicians have lobbied for input into legislation. Thus, the American Medical Association Amendment was a feature of both the Regional Medical Program and the Partnership for Health; and physicians in their private offices escaped the subjection to certificate of need regulations that industry sought for them.

Third, physicians have resisted external control by attempting to dominate regulatory bodies mandated by legislation, such as PSROs and HSAs. Fourth, they attempted to enforce sanctions against nontraditional colleagues, those physicians who attempted to organize alternative health care delivery programs, such as health maintenance organizations.

It should be noted that the major focus of these struggles has been the structure and control of the health care sector, not a simple attempt by physicians to maintain fees at a high level. The AMA did not take a position against the freezing of physicians' fees in the early 1970's. For the most part, physicians' fees, although they are handsome and rising, have not been under attack because they are not seen as the cause of radical cost increases in health care. That role is assigned to the assumed overutilization of costly resources.

It is because physicians prescribe this utilization that they are under attack, not because their fees are high.

It follows that physicians' fees will be maintained at a high level by initiatives taken by either industry or government, thus diminishing professional opposition to some extent and further fostering the image of physicians as primarily concerned with their incomes rather than their patients. That is, physicians will be seen as willing to go along with cuts in facilities and services as long as their incomes are maintained.

An indicator of the success and permanence of the new structural forms within health care is the extent to which physicians have been integrated into them, to the point of becoming their own managers and bureaucrats. Although they fought PSROs and HMOs bitterly, many physicians now work for them. And since the Reagan administration has replaced PSROs with PROs, professional associations are now competing for the privilege of paying for them. Originally physician participation and control were thought to threaten the basic premises and goals of these organizations. However, there is now evidence that physicians do not inevitably dominate organizational needs and demands. At this historical moment, physicians to a very large extent are forced to adapt themselves to changes by structural mechanisms within the health care system itself.

For example, peer review is well established as a cost containment mechanism, even though its organizational form has changed. Economic sanctions, such as cancellation of federal funds for nonproductive PSROs, along with such rewards as private contracts with industry for those that did cut costs, caused many PSROs to make serious attempts to create and enforce utilization standards. Where that happened, the physicians working within the PSRO used the same language and made the same assumptions critical of physicians' efficiency as did other managers.

Similarly, although physicians still dislike HMOs, a growing number now approve of IPA-HMOs, which have increased faster than other models. And yet, even within IPAs, the most traditional of HMO forms, physicians have found that they must employ the same control techniques as do the more advanced models in order to be competitive and survive.

Even physicians not directly involved with PSROs and HMOs contributed to the further development of peer and utilization re-

view and statistical, computer controls; it was their practice decisions that were fed into the computers, which can only average out
their work decisions and correct the averages to the prescribed standards. This has been a major legitimating mechanism for enforcing
compliance with the computer's standards. Thus professional expertise legitimates the mechanisms of control by management against
the autonomous discretion of the professional worker.

Serious questions arise about what it is that is being averaged
through these processes. The decisions of selected physicians are increasingly based on computer standards and then fed back into the
computers as if they were based on knowledge and service considerations by autonomous, representative professionals.

This appears to be a process through which peaks are eliminated
and averages are consistently lowered. As this occurs, it seems likely
that the lowered rates will be used as evidence that physicians had
indeed been overutilizing services and their credibility will be undermined even further.

One trend within medical practice, the enormous increase in specialized practice since the 1940's, may increase even further as a result of these challenges to physician autonomy. Individual physicians and their associations may attempt to promote the image of
"super-scientist" through accelerated specialization, thus placing
themselves above the general herd, for whom they may set standards.

This trend toward increased specialization has been anticipated
by planning agencies, which have attempted to increase the number
of family practitioners and reduce the numbers of super-specialists.
It will be interesting to observe the outcome of this struggle in the
long run. However, in terms of saving the status positions of physicians as an occupational group, specialization, by definition, is un-
promising. As Terence J. Johnson and others have pointed out,
specialization undermines the ideology of the equal competence of
professionals and thus the credibility of collegial controls. The increasing fragmentation of medical practice inevitably undermines its
organizational potential, and sets individual physicians and specialists
against each other in direct, competitive struggles. This is the situation that existed before the AMA consolidated control over and standardized medical education during the early decades of this century.

To date, no structural forms have emerged within the medical profession to circumvent the attacks on professional legitimating ideologies. Even if one accepts that the superior knowledge and ethics of professionals are real rather than ideological constructs, they do not appear to provide an adequate basis for an organizational apparatus sufficiently powerful to withstand such attacks. Physicians appear to have increasingly adopted the definitions of reality of their challengers. Peer and utilization review and HMOs do not rouse the kind of self-righteous rage as they did under the more traditional systems. Thus as consciousness follows historical developments, the demise of the last of the free professions powerful enough to control their own work and escape the relentless standardization associated with factory production appears increasingly imminent.

Only time will tell how all this will affect our national health care statistics and the quality of our lives as consumers of health care services.

Notes

1. INTRODUCTION

1. "Health Care Costs in 2000: $1 Trillion," *Health Care Week*, November 6, 1978, p. 1. Cites a study by the Public Services Laboratory of Georgetown University, Selma Mushkin, Principal Investigator.

2. Paul Starr, *The Social Transformation of American Medicine* (New York: Basic Books, 1983).

3. Springer Reries on Industry and Health Care (hereinafter cited as Series). Vol. 2, *A Business Perspective on Industry and Health Care*, edited by Willis Goldbeck (New York: Springer-Verlag, 1978), p. 3.

4. Ted Bogue and Sidney Wolfe, M.D., "Trimming the Fat off Health Care Costs: A Consumer's Guide to Taking Over Health Planning," *Public Citizen*, (Washington, D.C.: Health Research Group, 1976), p. 1.

5. Series, 2:2–3.

6. Ibid., 2:10–15.

7. Ibid., 2:50. Pilliod has been very active in health planning activities at Goodyear. "At Goodyear, the chairman of the board is personally involved. While at first this was more symbolic than active, today Charles J. Pilliod, Jr., serves as chairman of the Business Roundtable's Task Force on Health and is an appointed member of HEW Secretary Califano's National Health Insurance Advisory Committee. The director of Goodyear's Washington office, Rudy Vignone, serves as chairman of the WBGH, a task requiring large amounts of time and resources."

8. Conference Board Publications, *Health Care Issues for Industry* (New York: Conference Board, N.Y., 1974), p. 10. This conference was made

possible "by the generous financial support of the Alcoa Foundation, The Commonwealth Fund and the Rockefeller Brothers Fund" (p. 9).

9. Goldbeck is a very prominent person in corporate activism in the health care system. In addition to the work listed above, he wrote "A Working Paper on a Private Sector Perspective on the Problems of Health Care Costs," submitted to the Honorable Joseph Califano, HEW, April 1977, following a meeting between Califano, Goldbeck, and representatives of several major corporations.

10. Washington Business Group on Health membership list as of January 1, 1983. Mailed with an introductory flyer from the group in August 1983.

11. Series, 2:11–13.

12. Springer Series on Industry and Health Care (New York: Springer-Verlag). Volumes 1, 4–9 were edited by Richard H. Egdahl and Diana Chapman Walsh. Volume 3 was edited by Richard H. Egdahl. Willis Goldbeck wrote volume 2 and was guest editor on volume 9. Vol. 1, *Payer, Provider, Consumer* (1977); vol. 2, *A Business Perspective on Industry and Health Care* (1978); vol. 3, *Background Papers on Industry's Changing Role in Health Care* (1977); vol. 4, *Health Services and Health Hazards: The Employee's Need To Know* (1978); vol. 5, *Industry and HMO's: A Natural Alliance* (1978); vol. 6, *Containing Health Benefit Costs: The Self-Insurance Option* (1979); vol. 7, *Industry's Voice in Health Policy* (1979); vol. 8, *Women, Work, and Health: Challenges to Corporate Policy* (1980); vol. 9, *Mental Wellness Programs for Employees* (1980).

13. Priscilla W. Laws, "Medical and Dental X-Rays: A Consumer's Guide to Avoiding Unnecessary Radiation Exposure," *Public Citizen* (Washington, D.C.: Health, Research Group, 1976).

14. Paul D. Montagna, *Occupations and Society: Toward a Sociology of the Labor Market* (New York, John Wiley and Sons, 1977), p. 174.

15. Reinhard Bendix, "Bureaucracy," in *International Encyclopedia of the Social Sciences*, ed. David L. Sills (New York: Macmillan Co. and Free Press, 1968), 2:210; Max Weber, *Economy and Society*, ed. G. Roth and C. Wittich (New York: Bedminister Press, 1968), pp. 1026–28.

16. Barbara Ehrenreich and Deirdre English, *Witches, Nurses and Midwives: A History of Women Healers* (Old Westbury, N.Y.: Feminist Press, 1973), pp. 16–17.

17. Weber, *Economy and Society*. Throughout this work Weber describes a process through which different groups, including professionals and bureaucratic officials, are able to establish functional monopolies by utilizing interlocking support from some combination of other sources that have monopolies based on legal force, religious sanctions, vocational claims, impressive lifestyles, and charismatic birth. This support is given in return for benefits of different sorts that function to further legitimate and increase

the status of the groups to which the payment is made, thus legitimating the legitimator and strengthening the entire network.

18. Betty Morrow [Leyerle], "Professionalism as the Accomplishment of Work Setting" (M.A. thesis, Brooklyn College, 1975), pp. 37–39.

19. Talcott Parsons, *The Social System* (New York: Free Press of Glencoe, 1951), p. 436.

20. Mary E. W. Goss, "Influence and Authority Among Physicians in an Out-Patient Clinic," in *Medical Care*, ed. R. W. Scott and E. H. Volkart (New York: Wiley and Sons, 1966), pp. 428–29.

21. Boston Women's Health Book Collective, *Our Bodies, Ourselves*, rev. ed. (New York: Simon and Schuster, 1971); Gena Corea, *The Hidden Malpractice* (New York: Jove Publications, 1977), p. 268.

22. Executive Office of the President, Council on Wage and Price Stability, *The Complex Puzzle of Rising Health Care Costs: Can the Private Sector Fit it Together?* (Washington, D.C.: USGPO No. 053–003–00255–8, December 1976), p. 131.

23. Series, 3:vii.

24. Ibid., 6:36.

25. Editorial, "The 'Market' is Beginning to Protest," *Modern Healthcare*, May 1979, p. 5.

26. Series, 7:9.

27. Ibid., 7:126.

28. Ibid., 7:130.

29. "Two Reports Identify High-Cost Patients," *New York Times*, May 6, 1980, p. C1, describes two studies, one by Christopher J. Zook and Francis D. Moore, M.D., and the other by the Rhode Island Group Health Association.

30. Ibid.

31. Series, 7:126.

32. "Hospitals Worry Over Fixed Rate Set for Medicare," *New York Times*, August 28, 1983, p. A1.

33. "Ford to Reduce Health Benefits," *New York Times*, August 5, 1983, p. D3.

34. "The Surprising Swing to Non-Physicians," *Medical Economics*, May 30, 1983, pp. 55–63.

2. REIMBURSEMENT POLICIES OF THIRD-PARTY PAYERS

1. John Ehrenreich and Barbara Ehrenreich, *The American Health Care Empire* (New York: Vintage Books, 1971); Paul Starr, *The Social Transformation of American Medicine* (New York: Basic Books, 1983).

2. Sylvia Law, *Blue Cross: What Went Wrong?* (New Haven and London: Yale University Press, 1976).

3. "Groups Protest Tax on Health Benefits," *New York Times*, January 1, 1983, p. A15.

4. "FTC Eyes Ban of M.D. Input into HMOs, Blues," *Modern Healthcare*, December 1979, p. 32.

5. "Ohio MDs, state settle antitrust case," *American Medical News*, April 6, 1979, p. 3.

6. "Blues, Controlled by Docs and Hospitals?" *Modern Healthcare*, June 1979, p. 28.

7. "Blues' Consumer Slant, Tougher Cost Controls, Strain Hospital Relations," *Modern Healthcare*, June 1979, p. 34.

8. Rosemary Stevens, *American Medicine and the Public Interest* (New Haven and London: Yale University Press, 1971), pp. 458–59.

9. P.L. 90–248, Section 1902, (a) (30).

10. Cynthia Taft and Sol Levine, "Problems of Federal Policies and Strategies to Influence the Quality of Health Care," in *Quality Assurance in Health Care*, ed. Richard H. Egdahl and Paul Gertman (Germantown, Md.: Aspen Systems Corporation, 1976), p. 39.

11. Ibid., p. 40, citing P.L. 92–603, Title XI, Part B, Section 1151.

12. Allen Dobson et al., "PSROs: Their Current Status and Their Impact to Date," *Inquiry* 15 (June 1978):113–28.

13. Willis Goldbeck, Washington Business Group on Health, "A Working Paper on a Private Sector Perspective on the Problems of Health Care Costs" submitted to the Honorable Joseph Califano, HEW, April 1977, p. 9.

14. Charles Pilliod, Goodyear, Series, 3:ix.

15. Goldbeck, "A Working Paper," p. 27.

16. Ibid., p. A8.

17. Ibid., p. 33.

18. "PSROs funding cut off," *American Medical News*, April 20, 1979, p. 1.

19. *Medical Products Salesman*, August 1979, p. 81.

20. "PSROs hearing scheduled," *American Medical News*, August 24–31, 1979, p. 3.

21. "Assess PSRO Status," *Modern Healthcare*, October 1979, p. 24.

22. *American Medical News*, November 23, 1979, p. 5.

23. *American Medical News*, September 28, 1979, p. 2

24. Ibid.

25. Quoting Dr. Kenneth Platt of the Colorado Foundation for Health Care, Series, 1:35.

26. *American Medical News*, September 28, 1979, p. 2.

27. *American Medical News*, December 14, 1979, p. 3.

28. "Limit Inpatient Surgery," *Modern Healthcare*, July 1979, p. 38.

29. *Medical Marketing and Media*, April 1979, pp. 10–12.

30. "What the Mediplans' New Anti-Fraud Drive Will Look Like," *Medical Economics*, April 18, 1983, p. 47.

31. "Requiem for PSRO", (1972–1982), *New York State Journal of Medicine*, April 1983, p. 687.

32. Dobson et al., "PSROs."

33. Series, 6:34.

34. Kenneth A. Platt, M.D., "Inpatient Quality Assurance from the Viewpoint of the Private Physician," in *Quality Assurance in Health Care*, ed. Egdahl and Gertman, pp. 120–43.

35. Series, 6:34.

36. Ibid.

37. Damm in Series, 3:136.

38. Ibid., 3:178, note 42.

39. Series, 6:85–87.

40. Ibid., 6:43.

41. Ibid.

42. Ibid., 6:v.

43. Ibid., 6:14.

44. Ibid., 6:15–17.

45. Ibid.

46. *American Medical News*, July 20, 1979, p. 16.

47. Series, 6:3.

48. Ibid., 6:40.

49. Ibid.

50. Ibid., 6:97.

51. Ibid.

52. Ibid.

53. Ibid., 6:41.

54. Ibid.

55. Ibid., 6:43, quoting Albert Ritardi of Allied Chemical.

56. "New Information System Could Serve as Reimbursement, Rate-Setting Model," *Modern Healthcare*, March 1979, p. 10.

57. Ibid.

58. Ibid.

59. "AZ Hospitals Tussling With Coalition Over Cost Cutting Legislation Proposals," *Modern Healthcare*, July 1982, p. 66.

60. David B. Young and Richard B. Saltzman, "Prospective Reimbursement and the Hospital Power Equilibrium: A Matrix Based Management Control System," *Inquiry* 20, no. 1 (Spring 1983), pp. 20–33.

61. "Special Report: If You're Not Ready, Walk-In Clinics Are," *Medical Economics*, May 30, 1983, p. 77.

62. *Modern Healthcare*, May 1979, p. 7–8.

63. Ibid., March 1979, p. 12.

64. *Medical Products Salesman*, April 1979, p. 3.

65. *Journal of the American Medical Association*, June 16, 1979, p. 44. Statement prepared by John E. Affeldt, M.D., President, the Joint Commission on Accreditation of Hospitals. It appeared in a question-answer section.

66. *Modern Healthcare*, September 1979, p. 88.

67. Series, 1:88.

68. Ibid., 1:92.

69. Ibid., 1:89.

70. Ibid.

71. The National Center for Health Services Research is a component of the Office of Health Research, Statistics, and Technology within the Office of the Assistant Secretary for Health.

72. *Research Proceedings Series: Consumer Self-Care in Health*, DHEW pub. no. (HRA) 77–3181.

73. Kenneth H. White, Health Insurance Institute, in Series, 7:79.

74. Rosalyn Weinman Schram, "Mental Health Employee Assistance Programs": report for the Institute on Pluralism and Group Identity (New York, 1981); Series, vol. 9.

75. Goldbeck, "A Working Paper."

76. C. Larkin Flanagan, M.D., James Mortimer, and Richard DiBona, Continental Bank and Trust Co. of Chicago in Series, 3:61.

77. Ibid.

78. Ibid., 3:63.

79. Ibid.

80. Ibid., 3:68.

81. Ibid.

82. Ibid., 3:68–69.

83. Goldbeck, "A Working Paper," p. 18.

84. "Paying People $500 to Stay Well: Does It Reduce Health Care Cost?" *Medical World News*, June 27, 1983, p. 21.

85. Ibid.

3. INDUSTRIAL HEALTH PROGRAMS

1. John D. Blum in Series, 4:60–83.

2. This chapter draws heavily on the following works: Nicholas A. Ashford, *Crisis in the Workplace: Occupational Disease and Injury*, A Report to the Ford Foundation (Cambridge, Mass.: M.I.T. Press, 1976); Daniel M. Berman, *Death on the Job: Occupational Health and Safety Struggles in the United States* (New York: Monthly Review Press, 1978); and John

Mendelhoff, *Regulating Safety: An Economic and Political Analysis of Occupational Safety and Health Policy* (Cambridge, Mass.: M.I.T. Press, 1979).

3. Paul Starr, *The Social Transformation of American Medicine* (New York: Basic Books, 1983).

4. Berman, *Death on the Job*, p. 4.

5. Ibid., p. 41.

6. Ibid., p. 79.

7. Ibid., p. 137.

8. Ibid., p. 85.

9. Ashford, *Crisis in the Workplace*, p. 394. Also Mendelhoff, *Regulating Safety*, pp. 11–12.

10. "Employers Face Large New Costs," *New York Times*, April 29, 1982, p. D3.

11. Ashford, *Crisis in the Workplace*, p. 88.

12. "Worker Access to Health, Safety Records Would Be Narrowed Under OSHA Plan," *Wall Street Journal*, March 5, 1982, p. 8.

13. "Employers Face Large New Costs," p. D3.

14. Ashford, *Crisis in the Workplace*, p. 41.

15. Harriet L. Hardy, "Beryllium Poisoning—Lessons in Control of Man-Made Disease," *New England Journal of Medicine*, November 25, 1965, p. 1188.

16. Berman, *Death on the Job*, p. 84.

17. David Kotelchuck, "Your Job or Your Life," *Health/PAC Bulletin*, no. 50, March 1973, p. 1.

18. Berman, *Death on the Job*, p. 84.

19. Series, 4:6.

20. *Health Care Week*, November 3, 1978, p. 23.

21. *American Medical News*, June 9, 1978, p. 10.

22. Series, 4:80–81.

23. "Manville Sues to Get US to Pay Asbestos Claims," *New York Times*, July 20, 1983, p. D21.

24. Series, 4:68–69.

25. Ashford, *Crisis in the Workplace*, p. 145.

26. Series, 3:145–46.

27. Ashford, *Crisis in the Workplace*, p. 544.

28. Series, 4:81–82.

29. *Forbes*, September 1, 1977, p. 66, quoted in Series, 2:28.

30. Series, 4: 66–67.

31. Berman, *Death in the Workplace*, pp. 182–183.

32. Series 4:74.

33. Arthur Gass, Industrial Hygienist, OSHA, in Series, 4:74.

34. Ibid., 4:81.

35. *New York Times*, February 3–6, 1980.

36. "Genetic Tests by Industry Raise Questions on Rights of Workers," *New York Times*, February 3, 1980, p. 1.

37. "Screening of Blacks by DuPont Sharpens Debate on Gene Tests," *New York Times*, February 4, 1980, p. 1.

38. *New York Times*, June 23, 1982, p. 12.

39. "Screening of Blacks," p. 1.

40. Ibid., quoting Dr. Marvin S. Legator, a researcher in genetic toxicology at the University of Texas.

41. Ibid., quoting Dr. Barton Childs, Professor of Pediatrics at the Johns Hopkins Medical School.

42. Ibid.

43. "Dispute Arises Over Dow Studies on Genetic Damage in Workers," *New York Times*, February 5, 1980, p. 1.

44. "Training Occupational Physicians: Suppose They Gave a Profession and Nobody Came," *Health/PAC Bulletin*, no. 75 (March/April 1977), p. 9.

45. Series, 4:50.

46. Ibid., 1:50–52.

47. Ibid., 1:60.

48. G. H. Collings, Jr., M.D., in ibid.

49. Ibid.

50. Berman, *Death on the Job*, p. 141.

51. Ashford, *Crisis in the Workplace*, p. 324.

52. Gass in Series, 4:76.

53. Ibid.

54. This section draws heavily from the essay by G. H. Collings, M.D., Series, 3:16–28.

55. Ibid., 3:23.

56. Harry Braverman, *Labor and Monopoly Capital: The Degradation of Work in the Twentieth Century* (New York: Monthly Review Press, 1974).

57. Series, 3:53.

58. Ibid., 2:49.

59. Ibid., 4:86.

4. HEALTH MAINTENANCE ORGANIZATIONS

1. Background reading for this chapter included Roger W. Birnbaum, *Health Maintenance Organizations: A Guide to Planning and Development* (New York: Spectrum Publications, 1976); David Mechanic, *The Growth of Bureaucratic Medicine* (New York: John Wiley and Sons, 1976); Conference Board Publications, *Industry Roles in Health Care* (New York: Conference Board, 1974); Center for Information on America, editorial staff, *Prepaid Group Health Care Programs* (Washington, Conn.: Center for In-

formation on America, 1976); Philip Jacobs, *The Economics of Health and Medical Care* (Baltimore: University Park Press, 1980); J. Warren Salmon, "Monopoly Capital and the Reorganization of the Health Care Sector," *Review of Radical Political Economics*, vol. 9, no. 1 (Spring 1977), pp. 125–33; Robert Shouldice and H. Shouldice, *Medical Group Practice and Health Maintenance Organizations* (Washington, D.C.: Information Resources Press, 1978); and *A Student's Guide to Health Maintenance Organizations* (Washington, D.C.: DHEW, HRA 79–3, Winter 1978).

2. Mechanic, *Growth of Bureaucratic Medicine*.

3. *A Student's Guide*, p. 5.

4. Series, 7:36–37.

5. Ibid.

6. Ibid., 1:69.

7. Ibid., 3:6–10.

8. Ibid.

9. Mechanic, *Growth of Bureaucratic Medicine*, p. 91.

10. Ibid., pp. 96–97.

11. "GHA on Cost Scheme," *Medical Marketing and Media*, December 1979, p. 12.

12. Mechanic, *Growth of Bureaucratic Medicine*, p. 97.

13. Ibid., p. 89.

14. The AMA judicial council overruled the county society's expulsion for lack of evidence of incompetence, according to *Group Practice*, "to avert adverse publicity" (in Series, 4:48).

15. Interview with Dr. Ross, *Group Practice*, December 1973, p. 17.

16. Shouldice and Shouldice, *Medical Group Practice*.

17. *A Student's Guide*, p. 3.

18. David Kotelchuck, *Prognosis Negative* (New York: Vintage Books, 1976), p. 366.

19. "The King of the H.M.O. Mountain," *New York Times*, July 31, 1983, p. F1.

20. These legal cases are cited in Arthur Bernstein, hospital attorney, "HMOs, Hospitals, and the Law," *Hospitals*, December 1, 1979, p. 35.

21. Ibid., *U.S.* v. *A.M.A.*, 317 U.S. 519 (1943).

22. Ibid., *Group Health Cooperative* v. *King County Medical Society*, 237 P. 2d, 737, Washington (1951).

23. *Hospitals*, December 1, 1979, p. 35.

24. These foundations should not be confused with non-profit, grant-giving, philanthropic foundations.

25. *A Student's Guide*, p. 3.

26. Mechanic, *Growth of Bureaucratic Medicine*, p. 84.

27. Series, 3:107.

28. Himler in Series, 3:107.

29. Birnbaum, *Health Maintenance Organizations*, p. 3.

30. Center for Information, *Prepaid Programs*, pp. 86–88.

31. Salmon, "Monopoly Capital," p. 132, n.22.

32. Ibid., p. 129.

33. "Health Maintenance Strategy," *Medical Care*, May-June 1971, p. 32.

34. Shouldice and Shouldice, *Medical Group Practice*, pp. 40–41.

35. Ibid., p. 42.

36. Series, 1:67–68.

37. Birnbaum, *Health Maintenance Organizations*, pp. 19–20.

38. Conference Board, *Industry Roles*, pp. 59–60.

39. Jerry M. Blaine, M.D., "Some Thoughts on Periodic Health Screening," *Group Practice*, August 1980, p. 23.

40. Salmon, "Monopoly Capital," p. 129.

41. "The King of the H.M.O. Mountain."

42. Series, 2:38.

43. Berman, *Death on the Job*, pp. 137–38.

44. Conference Board, *Industry Roles*, p. 59.

45. This represents the best-known model with the largest number of subscribers. "The six largest have some four million members, or 60 percent of all HMO enrollees, and include the Kaiser Foundation Health Plans, the Group Health Cooperative of Puget Sound, and the Ross-Loos HMO in Los Angeles. Most subsequent HMO development is either modeled on, or a reaction to, the prepaid group practice form" (Series, 5:22).

46. Ibid., 5:28–29.

47. Ibid., 3, Chap. 18.

48. Ibid., 7:38.

49. Bynum Tudor in Series, 3:71.

50. Howard Veit, Manager, Office of HMOs, HEW, in ibid., 7:30.

51. Louis J. Goodman, Edward H. Bennett III, and Richard J. Odem, "Current Status of Group Medical Practice in the U.S.," *Public Health Reports*, vol. 92, no. 5 (September/October 1977), pp. 430–43.

52. "Are HMOs Changing Fee-For-Service Care?" *Medical Economics*, December 24, 1979, p. 11.

53. The Twin Cities project had a number of business sponsors who are not listed in the membership of the Washington Business Group on Health, indicating that industry's involvement in health delivery activities may be extensive at the local level.

54. Conference Board, *Industry Roles*, p. 86.

55. Series, 1:69.

56. "Aggressive Payers Push Twin Cities Hospitals to the Wall for Discounts," *Modern Healthcare*, July 1983, p. 68.

57. "Will the PPO Movement Freeze You Out?" *Medical Economics*, April 18, 1983, pp. 262–74.

58. "CA's Rush to Form PPOs Shows Move Toward Pure and Simple Competition," *Modern Healthcare*, July 1983, p. 74.

59. Series, 7:52–57.

60. "AMA Appealing FTC Decision on Advertising," *Hospitals*, December 1, 1979, p. 24.

61. "FTC Eyes Ban on M.D. Input into HMOs, Blues," *Modern Healthcare*, December 1979, p. 32.

62. "Blue Shield-Pharmacy Agreements Not Exempt from Antitrust Laws," *Hospitals*, April 16, 1979, p. 20.

63. Series, 1:70–71.

64. Ibid., 1:71.

65. Ibid., 5:v.

66. *Group Practice*, July/August 1977, p. 24.

67. "CA's Rush to Form PPOs," pp. 74–76.

68. Terence J. Johnson, *Professions and Power* (London: Macmillan, 1972).

69. "Who Really Likes HMOs?" *Hospitals*, June 16, 1979, p. 97.

70. Series, 5:v.

71. Ibid., 5:41.

72. Ibid., 5:34–35.

73. Ibid., 5:45.

74. Ibid., 5:35.

75. Conference Board, *Industry Roles*, p. 99.

76. "HMO Scoreboard," *Group Practice*, July/August 1979, p. 9.

77. Shouldice and Shouldice, *Medical Group Practice*, pp. 40–44.

78. *Group Practice*, July/August 1979, p. 6.

79. Including "Ellwood's InterStudy, the Group Health Association of America, and the Department of HEW," according to Shouldice and Shouldice, *Medical Group Practice*, p. 51.

80. Havighurst in Series, 7:55.

81. *Group Practice*, July/August 1975, p. 25.

82. P.L. 94–460, in Shouldice and Shouldice, *Medical Group Practice*, appendix 2.

83. Howard Veit, Office of HMOs, HEW, in Series, 7:29.

84. "Say Staffing Problems Hurt HMO Progress," *Health Care Week*, November 20, 1978, p. 7.

85. "Rising Costs, Delivery of Care Dominate Discussion at Middle Atlantic Health Congress," *Hospitals*, June 16, 1979, p. 20.

86. Series, 7:33.

87. Bernstein, "HMOs, Hospitals, and the Law," p. 42.

88. "State files price-fixing suit against Cleveland hospital group," *American Medical News*, August 15, 1980, p. 3.

89. "Three cities targets of HMO recruiting drive," *American Medical News*, November 23, 1970, p. 2.

90. Ibid.

91. Ibid.

92. Series, 7:30.

93. Ibid., 7:38–39.

94. "Broader children's coverage urged," *American Medical News*, December 14, 1979, p. 9.

95. Bernstein, "HMOs, Hospitals, and the Law," p. 38.

96. Ibid.

97. "HMO subsidies come under fire," *American Medical News*, January 8, 1980, p. 1.

98. "HEW Promotion of HMOs Condemned by AMA," *American Medical News*, August 3/10, 1979; "Medical societies protest letters to Medicare beneficiaries advising them to enroll in HMOs," *American Medical News*, August 17, 1979.

99. "HMO Follows AWARE'S Discount Lead," *Modern Healthcare*, July 1983, p. 70.

100. Ibid.

101. *American Medical News*, August 24/31, 1979, p. 22.

5. CORPORATE ROLES IN HEALTH CARE PLANNING

1. Series, 2:17.

2. Ibid., 1:73.

3. Ibid., 1:75–85.

4. Ibid., 1:85.

5. Ibid., 2:16.

6. Willis Goldbeck, Washington Business Group on Health, "A Working Paper on a Private Sector Perspective on the Problems of Health Care Costs" (submitted to the Honorable Joseph Califano, HEW, April 1977), p. 29.

7. Series, 2:16.

8. Ibid., 1:85–86.

9. Ibid., 1:84.

10. Ibid., 1:84–86.

11. Ibid., 2:42.

12. Ibid.

13. "Hospital Execs Spend More Time and Money on Trustee Education," *Modern Healthcare*, January 1980, pp. 66–68.

14. *Modern Healthcare*, January 1980, p. 40.

15. Rosemary Stevens, *American Medicine and the Public Interest* (New Haven and London: Yale University Press, 1971), p. 510.

16. Indirect aid is provided through Medicare and Medicaid; direct funding is available from both mental health and Office of Economic Opportunity health centers and from programs through the Small Business Administration, Housing and Urban Development, the Economic Development Administration, the District of Columbia, the Veterans Administration, and the Department of Defense, according to Stevens, *American Medicine*, pp. 512–22.

17. Robert Alford, *Health Care Politics: Ideological and Interest Group Barriers to Reform* (Chicago: University of Chicago Press, 1975), p. 228; Stevens, *American Medicine*, p. 505.

18. Stevens, *American Medicine*, p. 505.

19. Ibid., p. 504.

20. *Hospital Update: A Comprehensive Review of the Growing Institutional Market, 1965–1977* (New York: Drug Therapy Magazine), pp. 1–2; Elliott A. Krause, *Power and Illness: The Political Sociology of Health and Medical Care* (New York: Elsevier, 1977), p. 190.

21. Krause, *Power and Illness*, p. 249.

22. Ibid., citing John Ehrenreich and Barbara Ehrenreich, *The American Health Care Empire* (New York: Vintage Books, 1971), p. 299; also see Stevens' discussion of this interaction between President Johnson and the AMA in *American Medicine*, p. 514.

23. Krause, *Power and Illness*, pp. 252–58.

24. Ibid.

25. Ibid., pp. 255–56. Also see Kotelchuck, *Prognosis Negative*, pp. 414–16, regarding provider domination of the boards.

26. Sylvia Law, *Blue Cross: What Went Wrong?* (New Haven and London: Yale University Press, 1976), p. 178.

27. Three kinds of activities are regulated by the certificate of need process: "1) investment in new plant and new beds, 2) investment in new services and equipment, and 3) expenditures for renovation and equipment to support existing services," *Certificate of Need Programs: A Review, Analysis, and Annotated Bibliography of the Research Literature* (Washington, D.C.: DHEW, HRP–0301201, November 1978), p. 5.

28. Law, *Blue Cross*, p. 179.

29. *Certificate of Need*, p. 5.

30. Law, *Blue Cross*, p. 179.

31. *Certificate of Need*, p. 3.

32 ."Federal expenditures on the operation and construction of medical services jumped from $2.9 billion in 1959–60 to $15.1 billion in 1968–69, to $20.6 billion in 1970–71, a seven-fold increase in eleven years. Much

of the public money feeds into private medical institutions, in turn stimu-
lating new construction and thus having a multiplier effect in the private
as well as the public sector" (Stevens, *American Medicine*, p. 501).

33. Ibid., p. 511.

34. Law, *Blue Cross*, p. 177.

35. Alford, *Health Care Politics*, p. 228.

36. Structural interests refer to "those interests served or not served by
the way they 'fit' into the basic logic and principles by which the institutions of the society operate," as opposed to "interest groups," which organize themselves and do work to achieve their ends:

Dominant structural interests are those served by the structure of social, economic,
and political institutions as they exist at any given time. The interests involved do
not continuously have to organize and act to defend their interests; other institutions do that for them. Challenging structural interests are those being created by
the changing structure of society. Repressed structural interests are the opposite of
dominant ones. The nature of institutions guarantees that they will *not* be served
unless extraordinary political energies are mobilized (ibid., p. 14).

37. "Medicine is a classic case of social organization of production but
the private appropriation of powers and benefits by a structural interest—
professional monopoly—which through professional associations has
maintained control of the supply of physicians, the distribution and cost of
services, and the rules governing hospitals" (ibid., pp. 14–15).

38. "HSAs," *Health/PAC Bulletin*, no. 70 (May/June 1976), pp. 1–15.

39. *Modern Healthcare*, November 1979, p. 51.

40. *Certificate of Need*, p. 3.

41. Henry A. DiPrite, John Hancock Mutual Life Insurance Co., in Series, 3:119–20.

42. "Planning law extension hit," *American Medical News*, December 14,
1979, p. 9.

43. "Market Should Regulate Free-Standing Services," *Modern Healthcare*, November 1979, p. 54. Interview with Clark C. Havighurst, Duke
University, American Enterprise Institute, and Federal Trade Commission.
Professor Havighurst is an often-quoted participant at the Center for Industry and Health Care.

44. *Modern Healthcare*, October 1979, p. 90. This issue carried several
articles in which John Horty figured prominently. He is a lawyer whose
professional activities center entirely around hospitals and the law. He is a
member of the American Hospital Association and the Federation of
American Hospitals, and in 1974 he helped found the National Council of
Community Hospitals, of which he serves as unpaid president. He writes
and lectures on hospital-related issues at meetings and institutions across
the country, including the Estes Park Institute, of which he is a trustee. He

was also the originator of the Aspen Systems, which publishes many works of interest to students of the health care system and of industry's role in it.

45. "Phonescan," *Hospitals*, July 16, 1979, p. 37.

46. Ibid.

47. Ibid.

48. Ibid., p. 74.

49. Law, *Blue Cross*, p. 177; Ted Bogue and Sidney M. Wolfe, M.D., "Trimming the Fat off Health Care Costs: A Consumer's Guide to Taking Over Health Planning," *Public Citizen*, 1976; Barry Ensminger, "The $8-Billion Hospital Bed Overrun: A Consumer's Guide to Stopping Wasteful Construction," *Public Citizen*, reprinted in Kotelchuck, *Prognosis Negative*, pp. 413–18.

50. Law, *Blue Cross*, p. 177.

51. David Mechanic, *The Growth of Bureaucratic Medicine* (New York: John Wiley and Sons, 1976), pp. 87–88.

52. *American Medical News*, March 27, 1978, p. 1.

53. *Statistical Abstracts of the United States, 1977* (Washington, D.C.: USGPO, 1978), p. 111.

54. *Modern Healthcare*, November 1980, p. 92.

55. *Purchasing Administration*, April 1979, p. 6.

56. *American Medical News*, June 22, 1979, p. 19.

57. "Health Analysts Ask if Nation Can Afford More Physicians," *New York Times*, May 7, 1978, p. A69: "Some health economists have estimated that each additional doctor entering the market creates from $150,000 to $350,000 in health care spending annually. The number of doctors is growing more than three times faster than the population. . . . Uwe E. Reinhardt, a widely respected health economist at Princeton University, contends that the surest way to cut down the nation's health care spending would be to limit the number of doctors. That is a view shared by a growing number of health-care analysts and even some numbers of the medical profession."

58. Krause, *Power and Illness*, p. 288.

59. Law, *Blue Cross*, p. 179, note.

60. Alford, *Health Care Politics*, p. 14.

61. Krause, *Power and Illness*, p. 245.

62. Ibid.

63. Series, 2:15.

64. Ibid., 2:15–19.

65. Ibid.

66. Series, 2:19.

67. Ibid., 2:22.

68. Ibid.

69. Ibid., 1:79.

70. Ibid.

71. Ibid.

72. Ibid., 1:81–82.

73. Ibid.

74. Ibid.; Conference Board Publications, *Industry Roles in Health Care* (New York: Conference Board, 1974), pp. 72–105. *Industry Roles in Health Care* reports corporate involvement in health care planning with a number and variety of goals, including the creation of HMOs, cost containment, and creation of comprehensive health planning programs.

75. Series, 1:82.

76. Ibid.

77. Ibid.

78. Ibid., 7:106.

79. *Modern Healthcare*, September 1980, p. 7.

80. Series, 7:118–22.

81. Ibid.

82. Ibid.

83. Ibid.

6. PROVIDER ADAPTATIONS TO STRUCTURAL PRESSURES

1. *Hospitals*, April 16, 1979, p. 79.

2. Paul W. Earle, Executive Director of the Voluntary Effort in Series, 7:81–82.

3. Ibid., 7:43.

4. Ibid., 7:23.

5. Ibid., 7:6–7.

6. George A. Hensarling, Director of Employee Benefits, U.S. Steel Corporation, in *American Medical News*, January 11, 1980, p. 14.

7. *American Medical News*, September 28, 1979, p. 1.

8. *American Medical News*, January 11, 1980, p. 14.

9. Series, 7:14.

10. Ibid., 2:10–11.

11. Ibid., 7:56.

12. Ibid.

13. *Hospitals*, May 1, 1979, p. 2.

14. Ibid.

15. Series, 7:81.

16. Ibid., 7:97.

17. "VE: Some Health Care Administrators Skeptical," *Health Care Week*, October 16, 1978, p. 1.

18. Series, 7:23.

19. Ibid., 7:44.

20. *Modern Healthcare*, August 1978, p. 1.

21. *Hospitals*, April 16, 1979, p. 81.

22. The AMA developed and sent to 335,000 members a cost-fee index so physicians could compare their fees with the national average and other economic trends, such as the inflation rate (*Modern Healthcare*, January 1980, p. 26).

23. *American Medical News*, July 27, 1979, p. 17.

24. Ibid., August 24–31, 1979, p. 20.

25. *Emergency Department News*, December 1979, p. 8.

26. *American Medical News*, June 22, 1979, p. 1.

27. *Hospitals*, May 1, 1979, p. 82.

28. The American Hospital Association represents all categories of hospitals. "The hospital market consists of more than 7307 institutions. Over 97 percent are registered by the AHA" (*Medical Marketing and Media*, September 1979, pp. 24–25). The National Council of Community Hospitals represents non-profit community hospitals, and the Federation of American Hospitals represents investor-owned hospitals.

29. *Modern Healthcare*, July 1979, pp. 52–54.

30. Ibid., p. 54.

31. Series, 7:84.

32. Information about multi-institutional systems was drawn largely from Diana Barrett, *Multihospital Systems: The Process of Development* (Cambridge, Mass.: Oelgeschlager, Gunn and Hain, Publishers, 1980); and Montague Brown and Barbara P. McCool, eds., *Multihospital Systems: Strategies for Organization and Management* (Germantown, Md.: Aspen Systems Corporation, 1980).

33. The most commonly shared clinical services are blood bank, laboratory/pathology, and radiology. Others include anesthesiology and employee health services (Elworth Taylor, "Survey Shows Who Is Sharing Which Services," *Hospitals*, September 16, 1979, pp. 147–52).

34. "AHS Studies Service Effectiveness," *Modern Healthcare*, May 1979, p. 52.

35. "Shared Services and Purchasing Groups Rapidly Expand Programs," *Modern Healthcare*, September 1980, p. 10.

36. "Tax-Exempt Multihospital Systems Increase Services, Market Share," *Modern Healthcare*, October 1979, pp. 12–13.

37. "Billion-Dollar Humana Appears to be Ready to Start Buying Hospitals Again," *Modern Healthcare*, September 1979, p. 46.

38. Ibid.

39. Ibid.

40. "Humana Leads Way in Multihospital Marketing," *Modern Healthcare*, September 1979, pp. 47–50: interview with Wendell Cherry, LLC.

41. Ibid.

42. "Report on Hospitals Say High Charges, Extra Services Help Chains Make Money," *Wall Street Journal*, August 11, 1983, p. 6.

43. "Fifteen multihospital systems have begun offering unbundled services under affiliation agreements within the last two years. Systems of all sizes are getting into the business. Twenty-five of those systems that responded to the question in *Modern Healthcare*'s multihospital system survey . . . have added affiliation contracts within the last five years" (*Modern Healthcare*, August 1980, p. 92).

44. Cited in "Multi-institutional Arrangements: Shared Services Gain Support," *Hospitals*, April 1, 1978, p. 131. Elworth Taylor is Senior Staff Specialist, Center for Multi-Hospital Systems and Shared Services Organizations, American Hospital Association.

45. Taylor, "Survey Shows Who Is Sharing," pp. 147–52.

46. Diana Barrett, "Multihospital Systems: The Process of Development," *Health Care Management Review*, vol. 4, no. 3 (Summer 1979), pp. 49–59, in Brown and McCool, *Multihospital Systems*, pp. 57–74.

47. *Modern Healthcare*, May 1979, p. 73.

48. For example, see Steven G. Hillestad, "Multihospital Groups Need Marketing," *Modern Healthcare*, March 1979, p. 59.

49. M. Brown, "Multi-Institutional Arrangements, Shared Services Gain Support," in Brown and McCool, *Multihospital Systems*, pp. 43–52.

50. Brown and McCool, *Multihospital Systems*, p. xiii.

51. "Multiunits Given Discount on AHA Aggregate Dues," *Modern Healthcare*, October 1979, p. 26.

52. Williamson is also Senior Vice President for Hospital Corporation of America, Nashville, one of the largest investor-owned hospital management systems in the country.

53. "Multiunits Given Discount . . . ," p. 26.

54. Frost and Sullivan, "The Proprietary Hospital and Associated Services Market," cited in *Medical Products Salesman*, April 1979, p. 35.

55. *Modern Healthcare*, October 1979, p. 26.

56. Ibid., March 1979, p. 38.

57. Charles Perrow, *Complex Organizations* (Glenview, Ill.: Scott, Foresman, 1972), pp. 179–80.

58. "Chains Expecting Hefty Earnings Gains in 1980," *Modern Healthcare*, January 1980, p. 75.

59. "Dialysis Reimbursement Squeeze Spurs New Management Services," *Modern Healthcare*, August 1980, p. 80.

60. "Feds Finalizing Payment Cuts for Dialysis," *Medical World News*, April 25, 1983, p. 27.

61. Brown and McCool, *Multihospital Systems*, p. 55.

62. Ibid.

63. *Modern Healthcare*, March 1979, p. 16.

64. Dean Grant, "Pressure on Hospitals, Physicians Speeds Revision of Old Contracts," *Modern Healthcare*, August 1980, p. 72. These management contracts "typically involve pathologists, radiologists, nuclear physicians, anesthesiologists and emergency care physicians. They are almost exclusively dependent on the hospitals' facilities, staff and patient loads for their practices."

65. Ibid.

66. Ibid.

67. Ibid.

68. Ibid.

69. Ibid.

70. Ibid.

71. Robin E. MacStravic, Oh.D., "Many Benefits Possible with Vertical Systems," *Hospitals*, December 16, 1980, p. 76.

72. "University Hospitals Will Anchor Vertical Systems," *Modern Healthcare*, December 1979, p. 50.

73. Ibid.

74. "Standards Boost EMS Categorization, *Modern Healthcare*, May 1979, p. 4.

Bibliography

BOOKS AND RESEARCH PAPERS

Abrahamsson, Bengt. *Bureaucracy or Participation: The Logic of Organization.* Beverly Hills: Sage Pubs., 1977.

Alford, Robert. *Health Care Politics: Ideological and Interest Group Barriers to Reform.* Chicago: University of Chicago Press, 1975.

Ashford, Nicholas A. *Crisis in the Workplace: Occupational Disease and Injury.* A Report to the Ford Foundation. Cambridge, Mass.: M.I.T. Press, 1976.

Barrett, Diana. *Multihospital Systems: The Process of Development.* Cambridge, Mass.: Oelgeschlager, Gunn and Hain, Publishers, 1980.

Bendix, Reinhard, "Bureaucracy." In David L. Sills, ed., *International Encyclopedia of the Social Sciences*, vol. 2. New York: Macmillan Co. and Free Press, 1968.

Berman, Daniel. *Death on the Job: Occupational Health and Safety Struggles in the United States.* New York: Monthly Review Press, 1978.

Birnbaum, Roger W. *Health Maintenance Organizations: A Guide to Planning and Development.* New York: Spectrum Publications, 1976.

Bogue, Ted, and Wolfe, Sidney M. "Trimming the Fat off Health Care Costs: A Consumer's Guide to Taking Over Health Planning." In *Public Citizen.* Washington, D.C.: Health Research Group, 1976.

Boston Women's Health Book Collective. *Our Bodies, Ourselves.* Revised edition. New York: Simon and Schuster, 1971.

Braverman, Harry. *Labor and Monopoly Capital: The Degradation of Work in the Twentieth Century.* New York: Monthly Review Press, 1974.

Brodeur, Paul. *Expendable Americans*. New York: Viking, 1974.

Brown, Montague, and McCool, Barbara P., eds. *Multihospital Systems: Strategies for Organization and Management*. Germantown, Md.: Aspen Systems Corporation, 1980.

Center for Information on America, editorial staff. *Prepaid Group Health Care Programs*. Washington, Conn.: Center for Information on America, 1976.

Certificate of Need Programs: A Review, Analysis, and Annotated Bibliography of the Research Literature. Washington, D.C.: DHEW HRP-0301201, November 1978.

Conference Board Publications. New York: Conference Board:
  Business Leadership in Social Change, 1971.
  Health Care Issues for Industry, 1974.
  Industry Roles in Health Care, 1974.
  National Health Insurance and Corporate Benefit Plans, 1974.
  Top Executives View Health Care Issues, 1972.

Corea, Gena. *The Hidden Malpractice*. New York: Jove Publications, 1971.

Eastman, Crystal. *Work, Accidents and the Law*. New York: Russell Sage Foundation, 1910.

Egdahl, Richard H., and Gertman, Paul, eds. *Quality Assurance in Health Care*. Germantown, Md.: Aspen Systems Corporation, 1976.

Ehrenreich, Barbara, and English, Deirdre. *Witches, Nurses and Midwives: A History of Women Healers*. Old Westbury, N.Y.: Feminist Press, 1973.

Ehrenreich, John, and Ehrenreich, Barbara. *The American Health Care Empire*. New York: Vintage Books, 1971.

Enthoven, Alain. *Health Plan*. Reading, Mass.: Addison Wesley, 1980.

Executive Office of the President, Council on Wage and Price Stability. *The Complex Puzzle of Rising Health Care Costs: Can the Private Sector Fit It Together?* Washington, D.C.: USGPO No. 053–003–00255–8, December 1976.

Follman, Joseph F. *The Economics of Industrial Health: History, Theory and Practice*. New York: AMACOM, a division of the American Management Association, 1978.

Freidson, Eliot. *The Hospital in Modern Society: A Study of Professional Social Control*. New York: Free Press, 1963.

————. *Profession of Medicine: A Study in the Sociology of Applied Knowledge*. New York: Dodd, Mead, 1970.

————. *Professional Dominance: The Social Structure of Medical Care*. New York: Atherton Press, 1970.

Fuchs, Victor R. *Who Shall Live: Health, Economics and Social Choice*. New York: Basic Books, 1974.

Glaser, William A. *Paying the Doctor: Systems of Remuneration and Their Effects*. Baltimore: Johns Hopkins University Press, 1970.

Goss, Mary E. W. "Organizational Analysis." In Robert K. Merton et al., eds., *Sociology Today*. New York: Basic Books, 1959.

———. "Influence and Authority Among Physicians in an Out-Patient Clinic." In R. W. Scott and E. H. Volkart, eds., *Medical Care*. New York: Wiley and Sons, 1966.

Gouldner, Alvin W. *Patterns of Industrial Bureaucracy*. New York: Free Press of Glencoe, 1954.

Greenspan, Jack, M.D. *Accountability and Quality Assurance in Health Care*. Bowie, Md.: Charles Press Publishing Co., 1980.

Grusky, Oscar, and Miller, G., eds. *The Sociology of Organizations*. New York: Free Press, 1970.

"Health Care," *Standard and Poor's Industry Survey*. USPS No. 517–780. New York: Standard and Poor's Corporation, September 13, 1979, section 2, p. H3.

Hospital Update: A Comprehensive Review of the Growing Institutional Market, 1965–1977. New York: Drug Therapy Magazine (undated).

Hughes, Everett C. *Men and Their Work*. New York: Free Press, 1958.

Illich, Ivan. *Medical Nemesis: The Expropriation of Health*. New York: Pantheon, 1976.

Jacobs, Philip. *The Economics of Health and Medical Care*. Baltimore: University Park Press, 1980.

Johnson, Terence J. *Professions and Power*. London: Macmillan, 1972.

Kotelchuck, David. *Prognosis Negative*. New York: Vintage Books, 1976.

Krause, Elliott A. *Power and Illness: The Political Sociology of Health and Medical Care*. New York: Elsevier, 1977.

Law, Sylvia. *Blue Cross: What Went Wrong?* New Haven and London: Yale University Press, 1976.

Laws, Priscilla W. "Medical and Dental X-Rays: A Consumer's Guide to Avoiding Unnecessary Radiation Exposure." In *Public Citizen*. Washington, D.C.: Health Research Group, 1974.

[Leyerle], Betty Morrow. "Professionalism as the Accomplishment of Work Setting." M.A. thesis, Brooklyn College, 1975.

McAteer, J. David. *Coal Mine Health and Safety: The Case of West Virginia*. New York: Praeger, 1973.

Mechanic, David. *The Growth of Bureaucratic Medicine*. New York: John Wiley and Sons, 1976.

Mendelhoff, John. *Regulating Society: An Economic and Political Analysis of Occupational Safety and Health Policy*. Cambridge, Mass.: M.I.T. Press, 1979.

Merton, Robert K. et al.. eds., *Sociology Today*. New York: Basic Books, 1959.

Miller, George A. "Professionals in Bureaucracy: Alienation Among Industrial Scientists and Engineers." In Oscar Grusky and G. Miller, eds., *The Sociology of Organizations*. New York: Free Press, 1970.

Montagna, Paul D. *Occupations and Society: Toward a Sociology of the Labor Market*. New York: John Wiley and Sons, 1977.

Mushkin, Selma J., and Dunlop, David W. *Health, What Is It Worth? Measures of Health Benefits*. New York: Pergamon Policy Studies, 1979.

Navarro, Vincente. *Medicine Under Capitalism*. New York: Prodist, 1976.

Page, Joseph, and O'Brien, Mary-Win. *Bitter Wages*. Grossman, N.Y.: Nader Task Force Report, 1972.

Parsons, Talcott. *The Social System*. New York: Free Press of Glencoe, 1951.

———. "Professions." In David L. Sills, ed., *International Encyclopedia of the Social Sciences*. New York: Macmillan Co. and Free Press, 1968, 18 vols.

Perrow, Charles. *Complex Organizations*. Glenview, Ill.: Scott, Foresman, 1972.

———. "Goals and Power Structures: A Historical Case Study." In Eliot Freidson, ed., *The Hospital in Modern Society*. New York: Free Press, 1963.

Platt, Kenneth A., M.D. "Inpatient Quality Assurance from the Viewpoint of the Private Physician." In Richard H. Egdahl and Paul Gertman, eds., *Quality Assurance in Health Care*. Germantown, Md.: Aspen Systems Corporation, 1976.

The President's Report on Occupational Safety and Health. Washington, D.C.: GPO Document No. 2915–0011, May 1972.

Research Proceedings Series: Consumer Self-Care in Health, DHEW pub. no. (HRA) 77–3181.

Schram, Rosalyn Weinman. "Mental Health Employee Assistance Programs: Competing Models in the Marketplace." Report for the Institute on Pluralism and Group Identity, New York, 1981.

Scott, Rachel. *Muscle and Blood*. New York: Dutton, 1974.

Scott, W. Richard and Volkart, Edmund H., eds. *Medical Care*. New York: John Wiley and Sons, 1966.

Shouldice, Robert, and Shouldice, H. *Medical Group Practice and Health Maintenance Organizations*. Washington, D.C.: Information Resources Press, 1978.

Sills, David L. *International Encyclopedia of the Social Sciences*. 18 vols. New York: Macmillan and Free Press, 1968.

Springer Series on Industry and Health Care. Center for Industry and Health Care, Boston University Health Policy Institute. New York: Springer-Verlag:

    Vol. 1, *Payer, Provider, Consumer*. Diana Chapman Walsh and Richard H. Egdahl, eds. 1977.

    Vol. 2, *A Business Perspective on Industry and Health Care*. Willis Goldbeck. 1978.

Vol. 3, *Background Papers on Industry's Changing Role in Health Care*. Richard H. Egdahl, ed. 1977.

Vol. 4, *Health Services and Health Hazards: The Employee's Need to Know*. Richard H. Egdahl and Diana Chapman Walsh, eds. 1978.

Vol. 5, *Industry and HMO's: A Natural Alliance*. Richard H. Egdahl and Diana Chapman Walsh, eds. 1978.

Vol. 6, *Containing Health Benefit Costs: The Self-Insurance Option*. Richard H. Egdahl and Diana Chapman Walsh, eds. 1979.

Vol. 7, *Industry's Voice in Health Policy*. Richard H. Egdahl and Diana Chapman Walsh, eds. 1979.

Vol. 8, *Women, Work and Health: Challenges to Corporate Policy*. Diana Chapman Walsh and Richard H. Egdahl, eds. 1980.

Vol. 9, *Mental Wellness Programs for Employees*. Richard H. Egdahl, Diana Chapman Walsh and Willis Goldbeck, eds. 1980.

Starr, Paul. *The Social Transformation of American Medicine*. New York: Basic Books, 1983.

Stevens, Rosemary. *American Medicine and the Public Interest*. New Haven and London: Yale University Press, 1971.

Stroman, Duane. *The Medical Establishment and Social Responsibility*. Port Washington, N.Y.: National University Publishers, 1976.

A Student's Guide to Health Maintenance Organizations. Washington, D.C.: DHEW, HRA 79–3, Winter 1978.

Taft, Cynthia, and Levine, Sol. "Problems of Federal Policies and Strategies to Influence the Quality of Health Care." In Richard H. Egdahl and Paul Gertman, eds., *Quality Assurance in Health Care*. Germantown, Md.: Aspen Systems Corporation, 1976.

Wallick, Franklin. *The American Worker: An Endangered Species*. New York: Ballantine Books, 1972.

Weber, Max. *Economy and Society*. G. Roth and C. Wittich, eds. New York: Bedminister Press, 1968.

Wilensky, Harold L. "The Professionalization of Everyone?" In Oscar Grusky and G. Miller, eds., *The Sociology of Organizations*. New York: Free Press, 1970.

Zald, Meyer. *Occupations and Organizations in American Society: The Organization Dominated Man*. Chicago: Markham, Publishing Co., undated.

JOURNALS AND PERIODICALS

American Medical News. Weekly published by the AMA.

Berliner, Howard S. "Emerging Ideologies in Medicine." *Review of Radical Political Economies*, vol. 9, no. 1 (Spring 1977), pp. 116–24.

Brodeur, Paul. "Annals of Industry." *New Yorker* (October 29–November 26, 1973).

Dobson, Allen et al. "PSROs: Their Current Status and Their Impact to Date." *Inquiry* 15 (June 1978), pp. 113–28.

Egdahl, Richard, M.D., and Walsh, Diana C. "Industry Sponsored Health Programs: Basis for a New Hybrid Prepaid Plan." *New England Journal of Medicine*, vol. 296, no. 23 (June 9, 1977), p. 1350.

Emergency Department News. Trade journal for emergency departments.

Forum on Medicine. Monthly of the American College of Surgeons.

Goodman, Louis J.; Bennett Edward H. III; and Odem, Richard J. "Current Status of Group Medical Practice in the U.S." *Public Health Reports.* vol. 92, no. 5 (September/October 1977), pp. 430–43.

Group Practice. Monthly journal of the American Association of Medical Clinics.

Health Care Management Review. Trade journals for health care systems managers.

Health Care Week. Weekly for health care admir ⋮trators and professionals.

Hospitals. Journal of the American Hospital Association.

JAMA. Journal of the American Medical Association.

Kelman, Sander. "Toward a Political Economy of Medical Care." *Inquiry* 8 (November 3, 1971), pp. 30–38.

Kotelchuck, David. "Your Job or Your Life." *Health/PAC Bulletin* no. 1 (March 1973), p. 1.

Mazzocchi, Susan. "Training Occupational Physicians: Suppose They Gave a Profession and Nobody Came." *Health/PAC Bulletin* no. 75 (March/April 1977), p. 7.

Medical Economics. Trade journal for health care administrators and professionals.

Medical Marketing and Media. Trade journal covering medical marketplace.

Medical Products Salesman. Official journal of the American Surgical Trade Association.

Modern Healthcare. Trade magazine for hospital and nursing home management.

Navarro, Vincente. "Social Policy Issues: An Explanation of the Composition, Nature, and Functions of the Present Health Sector of the United States." *Bulletin of the N.Y. Academy of Medicine*, vol. 51, no. 1 (January 1975), pp. 199–234.

————. "Political Power, the State and Their Implications in Medicine," *Review of Radical Political Economics*, vol. 9, no. 1 (Spring 1977), pp. 61–80.

Purchasing Administration. Magazine for hospital materials management.

Salmon, J. Warren. "Monopoly Capital and the Reorganization of the Health

Sector." *Review of Radical Political Economics*, vol. 9, no. 1 (Spring 1977), pp. 125–33.

Young, David B., and Saltzman, Richard B. "Prospective Reimbursement and the Hospital Power Equilibrium: A Matrix Based Management Control System." *Inquiry*, vol. 20, no. 1 (Spring 1983), pp. 20–33.

Index

About the Author

BETTY LEYERLE is Assistant Professor and member of the faculty of the Department of Sociology and Human Services at Fort Lewis College, Durango, Colorado. She was formerly a writer for the Medical Business Services Division of Blue Cross and Blue Shield of Greater New York. She holds a Ph.D. in Sociology from the City University of New York.